AF410552

This book is dedicated to my Author colleagues in the AFH group for their support and the spirit to enhance my writing skills, imagination, and dedication to pursue my passion to bring about a change in the education systems and implement reforms in Teaching/Learning methods to enhance the student's knowledge and skills required for the millennium.

REIMAGINE EDUCATION FOR 21ST CENTURY

EMPOWERING EDUCATORS, TEACHERS & STUDENTS TO RE-MODULE TEACHING/ LEARNING PROCESS TO THINK CRITICALLY, COMMUNICATE EFFECTIVELY, COLLABORATE PROGRESSIVELY & CREATIVELY.

DR. SAMPATH DANIEL

Copyright © Dr. Sampath Daniel
All Rights Reserved.

ISBN 979-888569873-3

This book has been published with all efforts taken to make the material error-free after the consent of the author. However, the author and the publisher do not assume and hereby disclaim any liability to any party for any loss, damage, or disruption caused by errors or omissions, whether such errors or omissions result from negligence, accident, or any other cause.

While every effort has been made to avoid any mistake or omission, this publication is being sold on the condition and understanding that neither the author nor the publishers or printers would be liable in any manner to any person by reason of any mistake or omission in this publication or for any action taken or omitted to be taken or advice rendered or accepted on the basis of this work. For any defect in printing or binding the publishers will be liable only to replace the defective copy by another copy of this work then available.

Contents

Preface

This important book introduces a framework for 21st Century learning that maps out the skills needed to survive and thrive in a complex and connected world. 21st Century content includes the basic core subjects of reading, writing, and arithmetic but also emphasizes global awareness, financial/economic literacy, and health issues. The skills fall into three categories: learning and innovations skills; digital literacy skills; and life and career skills. This book is filled with vignettes, international examples, and classroom samples that help illustrate the framework and provide an exciting view of twenty-first-century teaching and learning.

- Explores the three main categories of 21st Century Skills: learning and innovations skills; digital literacy skills; and life and career skills
- Addresses timely issues such as the rapid advance of technology and increased economic competition
- Based on a framework developed by the Partnership for 21st Century Skills

The foundational reason why we find it so difficult to rebuild school curricula around the needs of the modern world is that we lack an organizing framework that can help prioritize educational competencies, and systematically structure the conversation around what individuals should learn at various stages of their development. **Four-dimensional education provides a clear and actionable first-of-its-kind organizing framework of competencies needed for this century.** Its main innovation lies in not presenting yet another one-size-fits-all list of what individuals should learn, but in crisply defining the spaces in which educators, curriculum planners, policymakers, and learners can establish what should be learned, in their context and for their future.

As rightly said, by Richard Riley, Secretary of Education under Clinton administration -- "We are currently preparing students for jobs that don't yet exist . . . using technologies that haven't yet been invented . . . in order to solve problems we don't even know are problems yet".

This monumental shift from Industrial Age production to that of the Knowledge Age economy—information-driven, globally networked—is as world-changing and life-altering as the shift from the Agrarian to the Industrial Age three hundred and fifty years ago. Moving from a primarily nuts-and-bolts factory and manufacturing economy to one based on data, information, knowledge, and expertise has had a huge impact on the world's economies and our everyday lives. The sequence of steps to produce a product or service, the so-called value chain of work, has dramatically shifted. The ICT – Information Communication and Technology that is applied commonly in our day-to-day activities has become as prominent, which governs the results in all our achievements.

Knowledge economies turn information, expertise, and technological innovations into services we need, like medical care and cell phone coverage. This of course doesn't mean that Industrial Age work will or can go away in the Knowledge Age—manufactured products will always be needed. It does mean that with increasing automation and the shifting of manufacturing (and its environmental impacts) to lower-wage, industrial-equipped countries such as China, India, and Brazil, industrial work in Knowledge Age countries will continue, to decline and service-based knowledge work will continue to grow well into the 21st century. But that's only one of the big changes that have arrived at our doorstep in the early part of the 21st century. And these changes will continue to make new demands on education as the century progresses.

1. The world now has a truly global financial and economic ecosystem. This highly interlinked system means that a disruption in one part of the world has dire consequences to economies everywhere.

2. The growing disparity in the world between rich and poor leads to social tension, conflicts, extremism, and a less safe world for everyone.

Yet the biggest challenge to the survival of all societies is the strain we're placing on our physical environment:

1. The global population has risen multifold from early 1950 to nearly 7.8 billion in 2020 and this figure is expected to exceed 9.9 billion by 2050.
2. Despite widespread poverty, increasing numbers of people are rising into the middle class; lifestyles have drastically increased their consumption of the earth's material and energy resources.
3. Increased consumption is resulting in climate change and other threats to the natural world and its global life-support systems.

Adding up overpopulation, overconsumption, increased global competition and interdependence, melting ice caps, financial meltdowns, wars, and other threats to security, in times such as these, along with danger and despair come great opportunities for change and renewed hope.

One of education's chief roles is to prepare future workers and citizens to deal with the challenges of their times. Knowledge work—the kind of work that most people will need in the coming decades—can be done anywhere by anyone who has the expertise, a cell phone, a laptop, and an Internet connection. But to have expert knowledge workers, every country needs an education system that produces them; therefore, education becomes the key to economic survival in the 21st century, imparting the right skills, knowledge & infrastructure for smooth implementation to the entire population.

Acknowledgements

I wish to thank and acknowledge my gratitude to all my fellow co-authors in the AFH community for inspiring me to write on the education for the 21st-century learners, knowledge seekers, and skills required by the students, and I also wish to thank many friends for their support and contribution towards my research on the various finding of the methods followed in the international schools across the globe and the many articles published by the UNESCO and the Governments, which gives a peek onto the initiatives undertaken by many nations in the World, to further the children's education and imparting the Social and Emotional Learning for sustainable and harmonious living for all societies.

My special thanks to many teachers who have been motivating and inspiring me to write this book to decimate knowledge and new methods and practices of teaching/learning for a better future for our children.

Dr. Sampath Daniel
Entrepreneur, Consultant, Author & Ed. Reformist.
Mumbai, India
6th January 2022

THE ANCIENT EDUCATION SYSTEMS PREVALENT, WERE RESTRICTED TO THE ELITE & RELIGIOUS SOCIETIES.

Education and its relevance in the ancient world

The ancient education system that was prevalent in many parts of the world was different in many countries, mainly dependent on the culture and the ruling communities dominated by the elite and the wealthy class of ruling families. The education was restricted to a set of a class of people, dominated by the cast, religion and restricted to a few elites of the society, like kings, priests, and the higher strata of the society, who had restricted sharing of knowledge with other peasants to keep the difference and make common people accept the elite society to give direction and leadership to them.

The idea was acceptable to both the communities and the practice stayed for many centuries, which is followed indirectly even in this modern age by the politicians and bureaucrats to keep the common people as skilled or semi-skilled factory workers or peasants working in the agricultural production.

Education in ancient India:

The traditional learning schools were imparting learning in religious schools or temples for the expansion and benefit of the kingdoms. One of such schools in ancient India was called GURUKUL

India has evolved from the early teaching of-Gurukula system of education, which was limited to a few students who were accepted by the Gurus who taught Sanskrit, Holy Scriptures Mathematics, and Metaphysics. The student and the teacher had a strong bond as the students lived with the Gurus helping in all the daily chores. The drawbacks were many, with limited student intake, and the education was for the preferred community, with the informal methods of the education system, and no specific time of completion or curriculum and assessments, which are still prevalent even today in some countries like Eastern Europe, India, Indonesia, China and Myanmar in very small communities. They are mainly prevalent in orthodox religions communities of Christianity, Hindu, Muslims, and Buddhists

The modern school system was brought to India, including the English language, originally by Lord Thomas Babington Macaulay in the 1830s. The subjects were science, math, languages, and most of the teaching was classroom teaching. Other extra-curricular activities and the link with nature were broken, which was evident in Gurukula.

The early schooling was operated by the Churches, and missionaries from England, Scotland, Italy, and Portugal, some of such schools run by the Nuns from Italy. They operated the schools built by the Railways for their staff children, in one such school I was educated in my primary schooling. There were also many religious organizations operating schools for their communities. Even today there are many religious organizations operating schools for their communities, in a very restricted manner mainly operating in remote distant locations. All these schools follow the guidelines of the state boards or central boards of education for their curriculums and assessments, though they mainly focus on religious practices and teachings.

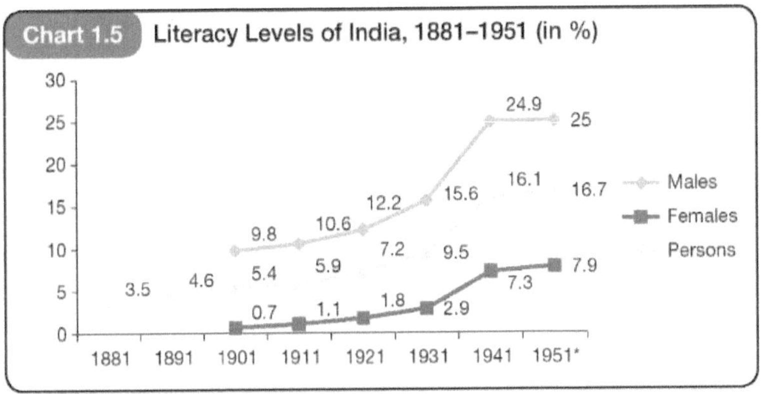

Note: (*) Data includes areas in Indian Territory only; for other years, both Indian and Pakistani territories are included.

Literacy Rate in India between 1881 to 1951 in percentages.

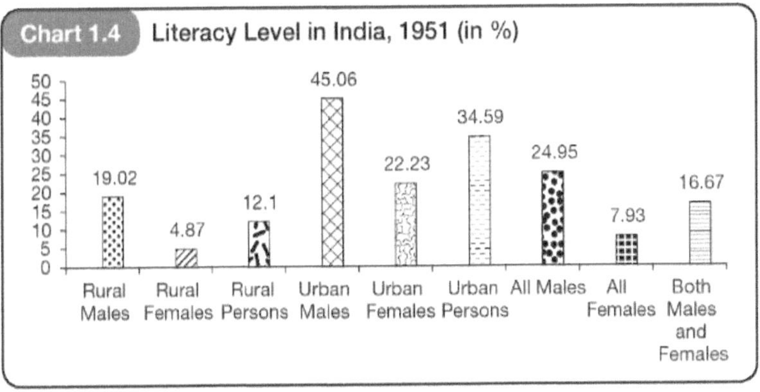

Education in India in 1947

After a century of school education there were reforms in school systems of having a unified standard of teaching in all schools with boards exams to assess the performance of the student, in this regards the Uttar Pradesh board was set up in India in the year

1921 with jurisdiction over Rajputana, Central India, and Gwalior, eventually by 1952 a new board was constituted in the name of Central Board of Secondary Education (CBSE).

It was the function of the board to decide on things like curriculum, textbooks, and examinations system for schools affiliated with it. Today there are thousands of schools affiliated with the Board both within India and in many countries like Afghanistan and Zimbabwe...

The primary education in all state governments is free, and under the constitution, article 45 Primary educations are the fundamental right of all the citizens. And the government spending in 2019 was around 4.1% of its GDP, which is very low compared to many countries that spend a maximum of up to 7% of their GDP, however, due to the Covid-19 Pandemic, many countries spending has dropped considerably, including India to the tune of 1.8% as schools were closed due to lockdown for nearly 2 Years.

The government in recent, proposed changes and brought about the National Common Minimum Programmers (NCMP)

1. To progressively increase expenditure on education to about 6% of GDP by 2028.

2. To make the Right to education a fundamental right for all children in the age group of 6-14 Years.

3. To universalize education through its flagship programmers such as Sarva Siksha Abhiyan and Mid-day Meals.

The Central Advisory Board of Education (CABE), continues to play a lead role in the evolution and monitoring of educational policies and programmers

There are also other bodies for key roles in developing policies and programmers, the NCERT – National Council for Educational Research and Training, the State Council for Educational Research and Training (SCERT) these bodies essentially propose educational reforms, curricula, pedagogical schemes, and evaluation methodologies to the state department of education.

There are different boards under the NCSERT, the CBSE board is set up for the central government employees children as their jobs are transferable the syllabus and teaching method is the same across the country which is called "Central Schools" or Kendra Vidyalaya, they all follow the textbooks written and published by NCERT, the CBSE has also affiliated schools in 21 other countries.

Similarly, another board was formed to replace the Cambridge School Certificate Examinations in 1956 which was run by the Inter-state Board for Anglo-Indian Education – (ISB-AIE) which is now called the Indian Certificate of Secondary Education (CBSE) there are many schools affiliated to this board mostly private educational institutions set up by the colonial rulers and the Christians Churches catering to children from wealthy families. Then there a small number of schools that follow the Senior Cambridge curricula which are called ICSE

To improve the overall quality of education, the state governments introduced A Comprehensive and Continuous Evaluation (CCE) System to improve the overall personality development of the student instead of the dependence on single results of the final examinations. In states like Kerala Information

Technology as a subject was introduced at the high school level.

The new Education Policy of the Government of India enabled is the emphasis on Constructivism; IT enabled education, Free Software, and sharing educational resources. - **References:**

Minute by the Hon'ble T B Macaulay dated 2nd February 1835
The story behind Macaulay's Education policy Part 1
Wikipedia: Central Board of Secondary Education.

The education system in other parts of the World:

In Mali - The Charter of Manden – (La Charte du Manden)

Dating from the 12- 13th centuries and established under the rule of Emperor Sundiata Keita of the Mandingo Empire, the Charter of Manden is **one of the oldestrecorded references to**

fundamentalrights, including the concepts of respect for human life, the right to life, the principles of equality and non-discrimination, women's rights, individual freedom, justice, equity, and solidarity. Passed down through oral tradition, there are two versions of the Charter, which advocates for social peace in diversity, the inviolability of the human being, along with education, the integrity of the motherland, food security, and freedom of expression and trade. Born from a context of the diversity of ethnicity and faith, the Charter of Manden provides guidance on how to respectfully and peacefully interact with other cultures and societies, thereby illustrating notions that are key to GCED, namely *respect for diversity* and *solidarity*.

Contemporary relevance to education:

The Charter of Manden is highly respected within Mali, promoting a message of respect, love, peace, and fraternity which has been cherished through the ages. It is widely seen to form the foundations of the values at the heart of Malian society. In 2011, the Malian government decreed the Charter to be part of the national cultural heritage of Mali. Also known as the "Kouroukan Fouga Charter", it is now included in the law syllabi of West African universities.

<u>In South Africa</u> - *I am because we are –we are because I am – (Ubuntu)*

Ubuntu is a humanist concept that means "**I am because weare, we are because I am**", speaking to how a person is a person through his/ her relation to and respect for others. This refers to an ethos for living together on the basis of care and respect, which is developed through the conviction that a person's actions have an impact on others and vice versa, and points to the notion of mutual responsibility. The idea of *shared humanity* is the strongest GCED notion within *Ubuntu*, where South Africans learn from childhood about the oneness of humanity based on biological oneness, spiritual oneness, and the recognition of common destiny. In addition, the concepts evoke respect for cultural diversity, peace, and non-violence, as well as human rights, through focusing on the interconnectedness and dignity of all women and men.

Contemporary relevance to education:

The values of *Ubuntu* wereincorporated into South Africa's 1993interim Constitution and its 2011 WhitePaper on Foreign Policy, "Building aBetter World". It is also referred to in theDepartment of Basic Education's 2010*Guide for Teachers: Building a Cultureof Responsibility and Humanity in ourSchools.*

<u>*In Oman*</u> *- Consultations – (Shura):*

Shura is a form of public consultation and decision-making inspired by Islamic practices. It refers to both a process and an institutional structure, namely the 'Majlis Al Shura' (Consultative Council) which is the lower house of parliament. It places value on taking a diversity of views into account, thereby promoting the notion of the **people's participation in thegovernance of public affairs**. There is a long history of religious pluralism and tolerance which can be seen clearly in the capital, with Muscat having two Hindu temples, one over 100 years old, and significant practicing communities of Sikhs and Christians. This cultural diversity and tolerance of pluralism illustrate the embodiment of *Shura* in daily life, as a process of negotiating differences, which echoes the core GCED notion of *respect for diversity*.

Contemporary relevance to education

The concept originates from the Quran. *Shura* is also referred to in the Preamble of the Constitution (1996, and its 2011 amendments). In civic education, *Shura* is expressed as Oman's political model. As detailed in understanding', and 'the world and its contemporary challenges.

In Tunisia - Freedom, Dignity, Justice, and Order – (Hurriya, Karama, Aadala, Nithaam):

Hurriya, Karama, Aadala, Nithaam may be translated as:'Freedom, Dignity, Justice, Order'. Theinter-related c *Karama* correlate to **values of human rights and fundamental freedoms, specifically the topics of equality and inclusion and justice** - echoing thecore GCED notions of *respect for diversity*and *solidarity*. Peace and non-violence - specifically with a focus on preventing violent extremism - is reflected in the concept of *Nithaam* ('order') or the rule of law, and is underpinned by a commitment to tolerance in and promoting tolerance.

Contemporary relevance to education –

There is a reference to a commitment to human rights, and human values, with the sources of regional civilization history and Islam, as well as global values, expressed in the principles of universal human rights and global human civilization in the Preamble of 2014 and philosophy, which provide space for learners to develop critical thinking. The system also supports the formal embedding of a debate program in schools that explicitly endorses democracy as a political system and promotes the Universal Declaration of Human Rights, inspired by the concepts of 'freedom, dignity, justice, and order.' In this spirit, Tunisia has established citizenship and human rights clubs, which emphasize participation and democratic culture.

In Republic of Korea - To the broad benefits of humanity- (Hongik-Ingan):

The concept of *Hongik-Ingan* is best explained as the guidingprinciple and ethical foundation of aKorean vision of an ideal existence. Theconcept emerged during the period ofthe oldest known dynasty on the KoreanPeninsula, the Gojoseon Dynasty (2333BC–108 BC). Dangun Wanggeom, thefounding monarch of

Gojoseon, putforth the idea which directly translatesas "**to broadly benefit all humanity.**" *Hongik-Ingan* suggests that the peopleof Korea adopt a spiritual outlooktoward life and aspire to the lofty goal ofbuilding a humane society in its highestembodiment of good. It is based on acommunal spirit that underscores the principle of well-being and love for alland is rooted in a vision of solidarityand volunteerism for the commongood. Although the concept cameabout as a founding principle of the firstKorean dynasty, it is seen to embraceall humanity, relating to the core GCEDnotions of *solidarity* and *shared humanity*.

Contemporary relevance to education –

The concept of *Hongik-ngan* can be found embedded in theNational Education Act, which statesthat "the objectives of education,under the ideals of *Hongik-Ingan*, thefounding philosophy of Korea, are tohelp all people perfect their character,develop a self-sustaining ability to attainindependent lives, become responsiblecitizens, participate in the makings ofa democratic state, and promote theprosperity of all humankind."

In Canada - *Multiculturalism/Interculturalism*

Multiculturalism is a national policy in Canada that seeks to ensure that "**all citizens keep theiridentities, take pride in their ancestry,and have a sense of belonging**". Central to multiculturalism is the idea that Canadians, regardless of race, ethnicity, language, or religion, are all equal. In the province of Quebec, "interculturalism" is most commonly referred to as the notion of "multiculturalism"– though not legislated in official policy – emphasizing the shared responsibility of ensuring peaceful co-existence. Both notions translate to a commitment to pluralism and *respect for diversity*. As stated in the Canadian Constitution, Section 27 of the Canadian Charter of Rights and Freedoms, "Multiculturalism" is a part of Canada's heritage. The 1988 Multiculturalism Act (MA) recognizes multiculturalism as a fundamental aspect of Canada (Article 3). All ten of Canada's provinces and three territories have some form of policy related to multiculturalism or human rights.

Contemporary relevance to education –

The 1988 MulticulturalismAct creates an obligation for thegovernment to promote interactionsbetween cultural communities (MA,Article 3). An important aspect ofthis work is carried out through theeducation system and the teaching ofother worldviews, and the cultivating ofsensitivity to the diversity of students'cultures and experiences (for instance,The Western and Northern CanadianProtocol – The common CurriculumFramework Grades 10-12 Mathematics).Another example can be found in theprovince of British Columbia, where,in 2008, the Ministry of Educationrecognized multiculturalism in its policyframework for schools.

<u>In France</u> - *Liberty, Equality, Fraternity –(Linerte, Egalite, Fraternite)*

Liberté, Egalité, Fraternité", which translates as **"Liberty,Equality, Fraternity"**, is the nationalmotto of France. All three conceptsare interrelated and are central to theFrench notion of "valeurs républicaines"(Republican values). The phrase *Liberté, Egalité, Fraternité* has been linked toFrançois Fénelon at the end of the17[th] century, as well as to the FrenchRevolution, when it was first expressedby Maximilien Robespierre in a speechon 5 December 1790. Taken together,these concepts echo the GCED notions ofclass, ethnicity, religious and nonreligious beliefs - on the basis of whichcan be built a *shared sense of humanity*.

Contemporary relevance to education

As the national motto,this phrase was written into the 1946and 1958 Constitutions and is a partof the French ethos. Inscribed onschool buildings, coins and even taxforms, *Liberté, Egalité, Fraternité* is partof the French identity and commitmentto create unity within and respector differences. These principles haveprompted the early provision (1881) inFrance of free pre-primary education asa means to ensure equal opportunitiesfor all. More recently, France instateda new moral and civic educationcurriculum (Bulletin official special n°6du 25 June 2015), which explicitly statesthat *Liberté, Egalité, Fraternité* are corerepublican values and, as such, shouldbe promoted through education.

In Bolivia - *Living well –(Buen Vivir)*

The concept of *Buen Vivir*, or "**Living well**," centers onthe notions of solidarity, generosity,reciprocity, and complementarily,related to the goal of social justiceand community, and referring to a setof rights related to health, education,freedom, participation, and theRights of Nature or *"Pachamama"*. Aholistic approach, the concept speaksto the diversity of elements thatcondition human thought and action,contributing to the search for 'goodliving,' such as knowledge, and codes ofethical and spiritual conduct in relationto our surroundings. The concept refersalso to caring for the environment, thusbroadening the notion of social justiceand well-being from the individualto include the community. Rooted inan Andean concept and found in the 2009 Constitution, *Buen Vivir* may be interpreted as a set of principles, such as dignity, social equity, reciprocity, and social justice, that are related to human rights. *Buen Vivir* emphasizes a broader understanding of progress and development, with special attention to nature. In these ways, this concept echoes the core GCED notions of *solidarity* and a *shared sense of humanity.*

Contemporary relevance to education:

The concept of *BuenVivir* shapes the vision and missionof the Ministry of Education, with allpolicies aimed at guaranteeing qualityeducation for all that supports thewell-being of the community. This visionhas contributed to the development ofa Base Curriculum of the PlurinationalEducational System, the elaborationof regionalized and diverse curricula,together with the participation ofindigenous and non-indigenouspeoples, and the training of teachersand education workers. Furthermore,the Ministry of Education developed theSectorial Plan of Integral Developmentof Education for *Buen Vivir* 2016 – 2020.

UNESCO's Initiative for common global education, sensing the rapid technological development in the World (ICT)

UNESCO has conceptualized the goal of global citizenship education to empower learners to engage and assume active roles both locally and globally to face and resolve global challenges and ultimately to become proactive contributors to a more just, peaceful, tolerant, inclusive, secure, and sustainable world. Global citizenship education has three conceptual dimensions. The cognitive dimension concerns the learners' acquisition of knowledge, understanding, and critical thinking. The socio-emotional dimension relates to the learners' sense of belonging to common humanity, sharing values and responsibilities, empathy, solidarity, and respect for differences and diversity. The behavioral dimension expects the learners to act responsibly at local, national, and global levels for a more peaceful and sustainable world.

Phenomenal advances in information and communication technologies (ICTs) have enabled people to connect and interact with others around the world anywhere, anytime. This has contributed to an intensified perception and reality of being interconnected and living beyond local perimeters. Moreover, increased transnational migration is making local communities inevitably more heterogeneous, increasing the need to learn how to live together. Tensions and conflicts among populations that have causes and impacts beyond national boundaries, and challenges for sustainable development, including climate change, also call for cooperation and collective actions at both global and local levels.

The Global Education First Initiative (GEFI), launched in 2012 by the UN Secretary-General, includes global citizenship education as one of its three priorities, along with access and quality of education. With GEFI, the world education community entered a new era in which education is expected to contribute not only to the fulfilling of individual and national aspirations, but also to ensure the wellbeing of all humanity and the global community. In 2015, global citizenship education was included as one of the topic areas of Target 4.7 of Sustainable Development.

The future impending concepts of the GCED (Global Citizenship Education)

1. Focus on the common values found in many local concepts as core entry points for GCED, including solidarity, respect for diversity, and a sense of shared humanity.
2. Widen the angle of GCED to explicitly include local concepts that emphasize peaceful social relationships and communities, as well as the environment.
3. Focus on the notion of "interconnectedness between the local and the global" when possible, rather than on the idea of "global", which is often viewed as not relevant at the local level.
4. Encourage implementation of the common values within the community, as well as beyond local and national contexts in order to demonstrate a shared sense of humanity.

This document was developed on the basis of contributions provided over the course of two months by three researchers, based in the Republic of Korea, the United States, and the United Kingdom – namely Darla K. Deardorff, Dina Kiwan, and Soon-Yong Pak. The work was conducted primarily through desk reviews of materials via the internet and in journal articles and books. When possible, informant interviews were conducted to gain in-depth insights into the concepts.

UNESCO staff working in Field Offices and technical personnel working in UNESCO National Commissions were also consulted for clarifications.

Acknowledgment & extracts Published in 2018 by the United Nations Educational, Scientific and Cultural Organization, 7, place de Fontenoy, 75352 Paris 07 SP, France © UNESCO 2018

CHAPTER II

EDUCATION AS A PURPOSE OF STABILITY IN THE 21ST CENTURY:

The Gross Enrollment ratio in schools is an important factor in every country

Continuously educate the entire population of the nation in the 21st century else, you will have 50% uneducated and misfit to live in the current world. Of this 50% (There will be disadvantaged Children who couldn't get the education and the balance elderly due to extended longevity of life, who could not cope with the application in the changing technological world.)

Within the education community, there is a growing trend to complement the discourse of access and quality of education with that of the content of education; to complement the discourse of cognitive skills with that of socio-emotional skills; to complement the discourse of skills and competencies for employment and the job market with that of skills and competences for learning to live together, and to complete an education that is focused on assessment with an education focused on relevance. The question of access is now complemented with concerns of quality and content. The world community is now asking if students are in school, what they are learning, and will it contribute to making the world a better place for humanity.

<u>Enrolment in pre-primary schooling facilities:</u>

SOURCE	ICDS/ANGANWADI	PRE-PRIMARY CLASS (FORMAL)	TOTAL ATTENDANCE
SAIES (2002-3)60 (3-5 years)	25.40	8.17	33.57
WCD (2009-10) (3-5 years)	33.57	NA	33.57
SSE (2011-12)	35.82	6.30	42.13 GER 57%*

Out of the different data sets available for the past years, the Report has used household survey data, rather than administrative sources, to estimate the number of out-of-school children and to generate profiles of out-of-school children. The primary reasons for this choice are that household surveys have data on both in-school and out-of-school children and on the age of the child, while the administrative sources give information on in-school children only, and at the school level. It is possible to use administrative sources for the estimation if data on an age grade matrix is available for all enrolled children in the 6 to 13 age group. Only DISE data attempts to provide this information but till Class 8 only. No information on children in the age group studying in higher grades is available. Household survey data are also more useful to analyze the profiles of out-of-school children as they provide details of the socio-economic and religious background of the children. Administrative surveys in India collect information on children "in school", making it difficult to disaggregate data on out-of-school children by child characteristics.

This analysis is mostly at the national level. India is a large populous country and states differ widely in their social and economic characteristics. Very preliminary analysis at the state level confirms a high level of interstate variations. In Bihar, Uttar

Pradesh, and Rajasthan, the proportions of children out of school are high in both age groups. But while the proportions out of school are high for both boys and girls in rural and urban areas in Bihar, in UP, the proportions out of school are higher in urban than in rural areas. Rajasthan, in contrast, shows very high gender differences in rural areas out-of-school proportions among girls are double that among boys. In states like West Bengal and Odisha, the proportions out of school are much lower in the 6 to 10 age group, but still quite high among both boys and girls in the 11 to 13 age group. In the states which are educationally advantaged, the so-called "last mile" children in specific social categories are seen to be out of school, and as seen from Gujarat data, boys from disadvantaged groups remain more likely to be out of school.

The analysis is limited by the unavailability of data on school participation of vulnerable groups of children in difficult circumstances. These children are likely to suffer from caste and class disadvantages, in addition to those caused by other problems unique to their situation. Anecdotal evidence suggests high proportions out of school among CWSN, child workers, street children, children living in slums, in migrant families, and among children in areas under civil strife. Lack of reliable data and correct estimates tend to underplay the urgency of dealing with these problems.

Source: SES All India Time-series, MHRD. The data are for SRI-IMRB surveys for 2005 and 2009, respectively.

School drop-out rates have been found to be very high among Muslim girls. Girls who are enrolled might be withdrawn when they attain puberty, or because of child marriage. As with other communities, Muslim girls find their parents invest more in their brothers' schooling than in theirs. Moreover, many parents are unwilling to send their girls to regular schools if they are coeducational or if they are schools without female teachers. Hasan and Menon (2004), in a major study on Muslim girls' education, point out those Muslim girls in north Indian villages are educationally much more disadvantaged than in other parts of

India.

These girls face various barriers including the deep-rooted patriarchal traditions in their local communities. The study found the lack of female teachers, and transport facilities to be important barriers for girls' education, but indicated that poverty is the most crucial issue behind the poor educational status of Muslim girls. The barriers to school participation of Muslim children, as identified in existing studies, are quite similar to those facing other disadvantaged groups, except that among Muslim parents there is a demand for Urdu medium schools, or at least the teaching of Urdu as a second language. More in-depth geographically focused studies are needed to understand why the proportions of Muslim children out of school are particularly high in certain states and districts.

Socio-cultural factors: Violence and sexual harassment in-home and community:

The global report on the impact of domestic violence on children indicates that between 27 and 69 million children are exposed to domestic violence in India. This report shows that such violence can adversely affect the development of children's brains and impair their cognitive and sensory growth. Primary school-age children who have been exposed to domestic violence show poor concentration and focus in their studies. A study by Plan India in four Indian states identifies the home as the source of the most severe and cruel forms of punishment for children. The survey reports that parents did not hesitate to accept that they punish their children physically and feel that they needed to discipline them. The forms of punishment range from kicking a child severely, inflicting burns on him/her, making the child starve, to assigning physically strenuous tasks. Both parents were found to mete out physical punishment regardless of gender. In spite of the fact that children seemed to take such cruelty in their stride, it appears to be likely that it would adversely affect their school participation and attendance. Public spaces in India do not provide adequate security to women, and sexual harassment is likely to constrain school attendance for girls, especially adolescents.

Economic factors:

The negative association between poverty and educational achievement is fairly well-established, i.e. households belonging to the lowest income quintiles are usually the ones with the least educational attainment. States with high poverty have the largest proportion of out-of-school children: UP, Rajasthan, Bihar and Odisha, and West Bengal. Again, locations associated with high poverty also have a high incidence of out-of-school children – rural areas for example, and to some extent urban slums. Social groups disadvantaged by tradition, history or politics also tend to dominate among the poor as well as in having large numbers of children out of school and this is due to the cumulative disadvantages that they face.

Costs of schooling:

For long years now the Indian state has strived to decrease the cost of education. At present no fees are charged in government schools. Additionally different states have been providing many incentives to make elementary schooling more attractive and affordable for disadvantaged communities: scholarships, subsidized books/ stationery, mid-day meal, student concession in public transport, etc. In some cases, residential schools have been provided in an attempt to bring down the costs of schooling further and provide a safe, supportive environment for children who may be living in remote communities, many of whom are first-generation learners.

However, the 2009 SRI-IMRB survey indicated that poverty/ economic constraints were the most frequently cited reason for children dropping out of school. This seems to reflect the fact that although government schools charge negligible fees, in reality, there are other costs of pursuing school education, which can act as a major barrier to school participation for children from poor families, these costs which include examination fees, books and stationery, uniform and private tuition, etc.

Effects of migrations due to economical reasons:

Migration is often a coping strategy for the poor, particularly in rural areas. The study conducted by Jha and Jhingran found that according to teachers, migration is a recurrent event on the household calendar of many children as their families migrate in times of scarcity. They either migrate to agriculturally more productive areas, to certain worksites like sugarcane fields, brick kilns, or salt pans (rural-rural migration), or to urban areas (rural-urban migration). Around 25 percent of the adults surveyed in the Jha-Jhingran study reported that they migrate and the percentage would be higher if young boys were included. Those who migrate with other family members often work on piece rates at brick kilns, stone quarries, orchards, sugarcane cutting, paddy or wheat harvesting, etc. Around 6 million children in the age group 0-15 years migrate along with their parents. These are predominantly nuclear families who take their children with them to the worksite, especially their girls (for reasons of safety) and their younger children. While it is true that some migrants have been able to spend their migration earnings on education, the poorest migrants who migrate with their families are usually unable to educate their children.

In general, migration poses certain special risks for effective school participation. In cases where the adult men migrate, there is an increased burden of work on the family members left behind in the village. Children need to do more household work and tend to drop out of school. It has been found that when the entire family migrates, the education of children is definitely disrupted, at least temporarily. In most cases of rural-rural migration – to sugarcane fields or factories, salt pans, brick kilns, etc. – the working conditions are extremely harsh and earlier there were hardly any facilities for children to study. Instances have been observed where not only the women, but also the children were expected to work, each according to their age and ability, or rather to the extent that employers can extract work out of them. The poor parents see this as an opportunity for the children to learn the work and many children become full-fledged workers by the time they enter their teens.

The barriers to education faced by children from migrant families depend largely on the pattern of migration. Migration can mean being away to a worksite for 7-8 months of the year, in which case the time spent in the village coincides with the children's school calendar for only 3-4 months. On the other hand, short periods of migration to prosperous villages in the vicinity allow children to remain enrolled in school, but with being able to attend irregularly. There are migrant families who move from site to site in search of work, retaining a tenuous link with their village. Children from such families may not even visit the same worksite again. So provision of schooling at worksites is not effective for this group of out-of-school children. Even recently undertaken field visits to Gujarat, Maharashtra, and Odisha reveal that seasonal migration is still an important barrier to the universalization of elementary education. Many children remain nominally enrolled, learn little due to continuous interruptions in schooling and eventually drop out.

Forced migration from areas affected by civil strife is also a major issue that affects children and their right to education. In these areas, families in large numbers are moved to neighboring areas or into camps, which render children extremely vulnerable to a host of deprivations and expose them to danger and insecurity.

Global Initiative on Out-of-School Children.

<u>Summary is for teachers and practitioners.</u>

CORE INFORMATION	KEY MESSAGES
Purpose (four capacities) The purpose of Curriculum for Excellence is to help children and young people to become: • Successful learners; • Confident individuals; • Responsible citizens; and • Effective contributors.	Developing the capabilities and attributes of the four capacities is embedded across all learning
Aim Curriculum for Excellence (CfE) aims to raise standards, to close the (poverty-related) attainment gap, and to prepare children and young people for their future.	Building on the messages of Building the Curriculum 3, the National Improvement Framework, Scottish Attainment Challenge and Developing the Young Workforce gives a greater focus to our aim.
Values The Scottish approach to the curriculum is values based. Wisdom, justice, compassion and integrity define the values for Scottish society.	Apply and reinforce these values at every opportunity to ensure children and young people develop understanding and respect for others and a sense of their personal and collective responsibility.

The curriculum framework	Building the Curriculum
The curriculum includes all that is planned for children and young people throughout their education. It includes four contexts for learning: curriculum areas and subjects, interdisciplinary learning, ethos and life of the school and opportunities for personal achievement. The Experiences and Outcomes (Es and Os) for each curriculum area illustrate the learning within each level. Curriculum for Excellence provides flexibility for schools and settings to plan learning suitable for their own context. The school community and partners should be involved in deciding how to use this flexibility. Children's rights and entitlements are at the heart of the Scottish Curriculum.	The curriculum framework, as laid out in the Building the Curriculum Series, remains the same. Teachers and practitioners provide a curriculum that is coherent and flexible, takes account of the local context and ensures appropriate progression and levels of attainment for all children and young people. The National Improvement Framework increases the focus on literacy, numeracy and health and wellbeing and highlights the need to close the poverty-related attainment gap. The Developing the Young Workforce Programme increases the focus on recognizing children's and young people's skills, the links between learning and positive destinations, and access to learning pathways that meets their needs and aspirations.
Moderation: Moderation is the way in which practitioners arrive at a shared understanding of standards and expectations. Moderation takes place at local, regional and national levels, including: • teachers and practitioners at the same curriculum level; • across a school or setting; • across a group of schools/settings; • within local authorities; • through regional groups; or • via national groups.	Moderation is integral to planning learning, teaching and assessment. The process of moderation is not an activity that happens only at the end of a block or year. Teachers and practitioners, with senior leaders, regularly consider a range of assessment evidence which demonstrates how well children and young people are making progress and achieving their potential.

Moderation:

Moderation:	
Moderation: Moderation is the way in which practitioners arrive at a shared understanding of standards and expectations. Moderation takes place at local, regional and national levels, including: • teachers and practitioners at the same curriculum level; • across a school or setting; • across a group of schools/settings; • within local authorities; • through regional groups; or • via national groups.	Moderation is integral to planning learning, teaching and assessment. The process of moderation is not an activity that happens only at the end of a block or year. Teachers and practitioners, with senior leaders, regularly consider a range of assessment evidence which demonstrates how well children and young people are making progress and achieving their potential.

CORE INFORMATION	KEY MESSAGES
Principles of curriculum design. These apply at all stages of learning with different emphases at different times. • challenge and enjoyment; • breadth; • progression; • depth; • personalisation and choice; • coherence; and relevance. Responsibility of all • literacy; numeracy; and • health and wellbeing. There should be a continuous focus on these from the ages of 3 to 18. Children and young people are entitled to two hours of quality physical education per week.	The principles are taken into account when planning learning for all children and young people. Teachers and practitioners identify what will be taught and how to best meet the needs of all learners. This is underpinned by a clear, shared understanding of progression and high quality learning and teaching. When planning learning, teaching and assessment Experiences and Outcomes are grouped or bundled together. Building the Ambition provides guidance to those working in the early learning and childcare sector. It should be used in parallel with CfE guidance
Assessing progress and achievement Assessment is integral to learning and teaching. It is an ongoing process. Achievement of a level: Achievement of a level is based on teachers' overall professional judgement, informed by evidence. Benchmarks: The Benchmarks are designed to support teacher professional judgement of both, progress towards, and achievement of, a level	A range of assessment evidence is used to plan next steps in learning. Assessment judgments' should be based on the Benchmarks for each curriculum level. The Benchmarks embed the significant aspects of learning and progression frameworks. They provide a single streamlined resource to supporting teachers' professional judgment.

Source: Calculated from SRI-IMRB 2009 data, population projections from RGI, 2009 and UNPD 2009 (2012 revision).

Definition 1: *OOSC are children who have never been enrolled in pre-primary schooling or above, and those who have dropped out from pre-primary schooling or above, covering both formal and non-formal education facilities.*

Definition 2: *OOSC are children who have never been enrolled in Class 1 and above, and those who have dropped out from Class 1 and above, informal education facilities.*

The differences in the estimated number of out-of-school children illustrate how estimates vary with changes in definition and methodology and bring to attention the urgent need for a uniform definition and methodology for estimation and population projection to be used.

The effects of the pandemic with drop-in GER in the past 2 years

Due to lockdown in many countries on account of the Covid-19 pandemic in the past 2 years, schools have been closed for In-Person classes; many have lost two years of education, especially children joining the schools at the nursery and primary levels, there were also many students in the final year of their schooling or graduation who could not finish their courses, their education success and their knowledge for work skills are lacking. Many Afro-Asian countries have suffered due to economic conditions due to loss of jobs in factories and service sector whereby they could not send their wards to continue offline schooling and also because of unavailability of net connectivity, lack of personal learning gadgets, the students were not able to continue schooling, and thereby the children are forced to work doing odd jobs or working in the farms with their parents, leaving the disadvantaged children out of schools. There are only a few private schools that were conducting Online classes for those students who have the gadgets and the connectivity in the big cities. WHO estimates, the total out-of-school children could be over 50% in many developing and underdeveloped countries, and also there are many children who could not attend schools in the past 2 years have lost their learning capabilities who cannot read or write basic languages and math, the current level of Out-of- school children are estimated to reach the levels of the past 10 to 15 years figures.

The statistics and charts are used, as per the predictions of the WHO and other world bodies, estimate that the children affected due to the loss of schooling and those who are the out-of-school ratio of the GER which is likely to reach the figures of 2009 -2012 levels.

CHAPTER III

GOVERNMENTS INITIATIVES AND SCHEMES TO PROMOTE EDUCATION TO ALL IN THE 21st CENTURY

Technology-based effective classroom transactions are needed

Over the years the government has mandated free and compulsory education for all children in many countries. However, problems related to teaching, maintenance of school facilities, and governance have impacted school quality. One of the important barriers continues to be the nature of classroom transactions.

Teaching methods have been slow to change and schools can become an unattractive place for students. Most of the children from disadvantaged communities are first-generation school-goers, and they need extra attention, as well as innovative methods of teaching to adapt schooling to their experience and context, with fast technological changes, and new concepts of teaching/learning, especially with the application of personal gadgets and 5G fiber connectivity to all locations, can make a big impact in education, this has now become a big challenge in schools, though the advantages and the content of learning are enormous and freely available on the web and has the advantage of teaching students in far and remote locations and imparting quality mass education for all.

The barrier thus is a complex combination of weaknesses in teacher recruitment policy, curricular needs of students from varying backgrounds, and governance issues, as well as factors such as lack of teacher motivation, non-teaching duties, and social distance between teacher and students.

However, Activity Based Learning (ABL) which has been implemented in several states has emerged as the potential pedagogical model in reducing achievement gaps in gender and social groups along with the provision of child-centered and child-friendly education.

Barriers in child education: The barriers faced by most vulnerable groups are immense. For children with special needs, major challenges remain by way of early identification of disability, sensitization of teachers and students, provision of adequate resource support for inclusive education in schools, and, most importantly, incorporating the true spirit of inclusive education. Street children constitute another group who face major barriers in attending school. Uncertain livelihoods and living arrangements, pressures to earn at a young age, and violence within slums continue to impact school participation adversely in the case of slum children, especially boys. The ongoing civil strife in some parts of the countries has resulted in disrupted schooling for many children. While the government is sensitive to this barrier to school participation, more effective action is needed. Many of the barriers to school participation can be removed with better governance. Decentralized planning and management, have made the planning process more inclusive but more needs to be done in this area. Decentralizations have led to a multiplicity of players in the education sector as SSA officials, officials of the state education department, and local body members all have a role to play. At times lack of full clarity about their roles is one of the reasons that hinder the efficacy of many government programs.

The demand-side barriers for girls in rural areas are relatively fewer at the primary stage of schooling, but play a major role in keeping adolescent girls in schools. Norms of child marriage are an additional barrier faced by girls. The supply-side problems arising from lack of upper primary schools in the immediate neighborhoods and the inadequate number of female teachers add to these barriers, to overcome some of these problems like child marriage in India, the Government has passed legislation to increase the marriage age to 21 years from the earlier 18 years of age effective 2022.

The challenge at present is not only to enroll all children in school but to ensure that they attend school regularly and complete at least eight years of schooling. The supply-side barriers are important in keeping children in school. Barriers in terms of school infrastructure and quality are relevant across population groups. But for the socio-economically disadvantaged groups who still face many demand-side barriers, the supply barriers add to the obstacles to school participation. These disadvantaged children are usually concentrated in specific locations – backward districts and blocks, remote rural habitations, urban slums, etc., where the supply barriers are more acute.

Many of the demand-side barriers have their roots in socio-cultural factors that are resistant to change. With the rural areas becoming better connected and with the government vigorously pushing the agenda of universalization of elementary education, enrolment has increased considerably, especially at the primary level. For children in the 11 to 13 age group, especially in rural families, the traditional norms of early entry into the world of work (for boys to contribute to family livelihoods, for girls to take on household chores/agricultural work), hinder education mainly in the Afro-Asian countries. This is an important barrier in both the rural and urban areas, though the extent of work participation by these children is underestimated from available surveys owing to limitations arising from the definition of "children's work and the nature of their work". In urban areas, the barriers are less challenging but boys tend to be more out of school in some socio-economic groups, possibly arising from more employment opportunities for children in the urban milieu and enforcement inadequacies of child labor laws.

Language is an issue particularly for tribal children living in remote areas since the teacher imparting the classroom instructions may be unfamiliar with the language spoken by these children at home. For a girl from a poor family, language may be less of a barrier, but social discrimination may be more acute. In the urban milieu, in addition to barriers arising from poverty and uncertain livelihood, children working and living in the streets and slum areas suffer access problems due to uncertainty of residence.

The policy response of the Indian government in the area of elementary education has been to address the gamut of the barriers to schooling through the successive five-year plans. While some interventions have worked better than others, it needs to be stated at the outset that just as the barriers to school participation are interlinked, so are the policy measures that address them. Improvement in indicators such as enrolment and gender parity is a result of a combination of several policies working in harmony.

Some gaps remain in access for some especially vulnerable groups of children such as migrant children, street children, children living in slums, and children in areas affected by civil strife.

Corrective measures to be incorporated: School functioning is expected to improve with the setting up of School Management Committees to monitor and support schooling, but their members need extensive capacity building to be effective. While elementary education has received considerable financial resources with the advent of the SSA, the overall resource availability for the education sector is still far from adequate. Fiscal constraints on the central and state governments have compounded the problem. The mismatch between need and allocation and slow fund flow continue to be major obstacles in project implementation. Financial management also suffers from inadequate staffing and support is required to enhance the capacities of the staff at state, district, and sub-district levels.

Strategy to adapt for children from low-income groups:

Children from poor families, particularly first-generation learners, require pre-primary education to acquire some level of readiness for primary schooling. A little more than half the target age group access the preschool facilities provided through Anganwadis in India, similar such pre-schools have been adapted in many countries.

Increasing access and quality of preschool education may well contribute to retaining more children in school, by giving them a more solid foundation in their early years of schooling. Access to schooling is less of a barrier to school participation at present. Distance has ceased to be a major reason even for dropping out, although it is still fairly important for rural females, particularly among older age groups. Access continues to be a barrier for some other groups of children such as children of migrant families, children from tribal communities who live in isolated and hilly terrain, street children, children with disabilities, and children in areas affected by civil strife. School infrastructure is one aspect of the government school system that has improved steadily over the past decades. But several studies have indicated the need for greater attention towards maintenance of these infrastructural facilities.

Education to mixed barriers groups of disadvantaged children in India:

There are schemes targeted at out-of-school children from specific disadvantaged groups, and they have produced mixed results. In certain areas, the Indian government has introduced KGBVs which provide free residential facilities and schooling for out-of-school girls from marginalized communities who are 11 years or above. Ashram schools for tribal children and hostel facilities for different disadvantaged groups have also been set up for children in remote areas. Parents have indicated a demand for these schools. However, evaluations suggest that these have had varying degrees of success and their benefits are limited unless greater monitoring of quality can be ensured.

The difference in language and culture has been a major barrier in the education of children belonging to ST groups. Several state governments have attempted to address this through the MLE strategy. These schools have been piloted in Andhra Pradesh, Odisha, and Chhattisgarh, and scaling up is in progress. For Muslim children, several schemes have been developed by focusing on special schemes in areas with minority concentration: modernizing Madrasas, and expanding schooling infrastructure for this community. But given that most of the children from this community reportedly attend mainstream schools, the impact has been limited.

Special needs Children's education:

Inclusive education policies for special-needs children have been introduced, which have shown improvement in enrolments. But here, too, the focus has been on the physical provision of inputs like ramps, and a lot needs to be done on improving the teaching, through the provision of teacher training of longer duration for the teachers who are engaged in mainstreaming mildly disabled children and through the provision of more teachers and other resources for inclusion of children with severe and profound disabilities. A greater degree of social sensitization of parents and the community (and teachers and other government functionaries) is also very necessary. Many of the demand-side barriers arise from socio-cultural norms and are difficult to change. Efforts at community mobilization have positively impacted these norms for certain population groups but not for all. Laws regarding the age of marriage, which is now raised to 21 years of age and adherence to strict child labor, implemented, would go a long way to change the norms.

Teacher Training and Capabilities:

There is a greater focus on improving teachers' capacities to lead the changes inside the classroom by revising norms of teacher recruitment and revamping teacher education and in-service training curriculum. In 2009 the National Curriculum Framework of Teacher Education (NCFTE) was formulated based on the National Curriculum Framework, 2005. All teachers, existing and aspiring, have to acquire professional teacher education. They are also required to clear a Teacher Eligibility Test (TET). However there is a lot of lacuna in implementing the recruitment scheme in the states, stricter norms of selection would improve the quality of education and the success of the students.

Robust Statistics are indicators for better planning and implementations of schemes:

The major role education statistics can play in planning, monitoring, policy formulation, and advocacy, the multiple sources of data need to be interpreted and used carefully. Small differences in definitions of out-of-school children or calculations may lead to very different policy implications. So it is important to have standardized definitions and methodology to identify and estimate out-of-school children. The definition proposed in the SSA in the context of Special Training for out-of-school children, that is, a child 6-14 years of age is considered out of school "if he/she has never been enrolled in an elementary school or if after enrolment has been absent from school without prior intimation for reasons of absence for a period of 45 days or more" is a useful starting point.

The following recommendations are made on the premise that this definition (or a similar one) will be accepted by all state governments in identifying out-of-school children.

1. **Need for multiple indicators of schooling:** The number of out-of-school children shows a sharp decline, but this single statistic indicates that school participation rate in the 6 to 13 age group has improved but does not indicate that many children continue to drop out before completing 8 years of schooling. Since multiple factors such as illness and low learning levels influence retention and age-appropriate learning it is important to collect data on children in school-related to their attendance and grade

completion by age. More information on in-school children such as learning levels, mother tongue, special needs if any, attendance, and age, which may influence a child's likelihood of dropping out need to be collected. This will help in diagnosing the reasons why the child is at risk and planning on its basis to bring all children to school.

2. **Need to harmonize definitions and methodologies:** No one data source can provide a comprehensive picture of the out-of-school children issue. In India, there are several sources, which usually highlight different issues. A major difference between data from household surveys and administrative surveys is that while the household surveys focus on children in a particular age group, the administrative survey focuses on children enrolled in particular grades. The indicators based on these alternative sources should be considered together for diagnostic purposes. It is important to ensure that the indicators built from different datasets are complementary and not contradictory. For this purpose, the definitions of indicators from different sources and, where possible, the methodologies used, should be harmonized.

3. **Need to monitor attendance:** The schooling status of a child may change over the year with changes in the child's attendance. So an annual exercise of community mapping may not succeed in identifying all children who are out of school. It needs to be supplemented by monitoring of attendance by school teachers and SMC members, and follow-up action. Such timely action may prevent some children from dropping out.

4. **Provide support to stakeholders in the use of education data:** Statistics on school access and infrastructure are useful tools at both macro and micro levels for planning, monitoring, and implementation. At present Report Cards on the basis of DISE are also available at school levels. But its use is quite limited at decentralized levels as the SMC members, teachers and other stakeholders need training and support to understand the potential use of the Report Cards and to use it for their activities.

5. **Need to extend the scope of Household Surveys:** To include children up to 18 years of age and to collect data from vulnerable population groups: During household surveys, education-related data on older. Children (up to 18 years) need to be collected. Existing data sources show that 6 to 14-year-olds are not all enrolled in age-appropriate grades and many children drop out before completing the eighth grade at 15 years of age or higher. Enrolment data of children up to 18 years will reflect the proportion who drop out before completing elementary education. Identification of out-of-school children is not easy, particularly for those in vulnerable groups. Clear definitions and instructions should be given in the questionnaire. Training should be given to identify children with special needs, and strategies should be developed to identify migrant children. Close monitoring of children from migrant families may be necessary. Similar strategies may be necessary to identify out-of-school working children, particularly those involved in seasonal work or part-time work. f)

6. **Need to extend the scope of School Surveys:** To collect details of children enrolled in grades 1 to 12 and to include schools of all management types: DISE data collected information on children in grades 1 to 8. Now under UDISE, data on grades 1 to 12 are collected. This is a useful step. For use in planning and monitoring, additional details of all enrolled children such as age, address, and grade enrolled in the previous year should be collected.

Enrolment data from all schools – government and private – should be collected. Care needs to be taken that no child is double-counted through this process. The enrolment registers should be maintained correctly by developing and utilizing standard record-keeping registers at all schools.

The school teachers should be given clear instructions and the capacity to identify a child who has not attended school continuously for 45 days find out whether the child has changed school or dropped out, and update the enrolment register accordingly.

As already mentioned accurate statistics will give the right directions for taking corrective measures and introduce effective policies to achieve the desired results.

CHAPTER IV

METHODS AND INITIATIVES TO PROMOTE KNOWLEDGE AND CONTINUED EDUCATION

Re-focusing Curriculum for Excellence

This definitive statement is for teachers and practitioners, including those in early learning and childcare, youth work, colleges, and local authorities. It will be important for teachers, practitioners, leaders, and local authority staff to consider how it applies in the context of their own stage, phase, sector, and local authority.

Curriculum for Excellence (CfE) is transforming learning experiences for children and young people across Scotland. The four capacities achieved in the implementations are CfE

- Successful learners.
- Confident individuals.
- Responsible citizens.
- Effective contributors.

The range of learning opportunities and the breadth of children's and young people's achievements are greater than ever before. In recent years there has been a great deal of very positive improvement work in early learning and childcare, schools and colleges on which we can continue to build. Moving forward, the two key priorities for CfE are:

1. Ensuring the best possible progression in literacy, numeracy, and health and wellbeing for every child and young person; and
2. Closing the attainment gap.

To deliver this focus, a number of challenges remain. There is currently too much support material and guidance for practitioners. This is contributing to the growth of over-bureaucratic approaches to planning and assessment in many schools and classrooms across the country.

Despite the recognition of these issues in the Tackling Bureaucracy report, progress has been far too slow. As a result, we are taking action to significantly streamline all our support and guidance materials for the curriculum. This statement and the benchmarks to be published in this session are key to this streamlined approach. This statement is intended to provide clear, practical advice for teachers and practitioners on planning learning, teaching, and assessment.

It provides key messages about what teachers and practitioners are expected to do, effectively plan learning, teaching, and assessment for all learners, and also suggests what should be avoided. Teachers should be empowered to use the flexibility that CfE provides to organize learning for children and young people in ways that best meets learners' needs. Schools should be working in a collegiate way to make key decisions. The appendix to this statement summarizes the key components of the curriculum framework within which teachers and practitioners are now expected to teach. Moving forward, the two key resources that teachers should use to plan learning, teaching, and assessment are.

Guide Questions When Making Your Own Lessons

Below are guide questions that will assist teachers in deciding the learning objectives,

Themes and activities to align with the needs of teachers and students as well as the

resources available.

1. **On student context:** What are your students' interests? What is the community like? What issues do they care about? What

are their motivations and What will make them want to use the lessons?

2. ***On teacher interests:*** What are you passionate about? Do you have causes that you think are important to impart to your students?

3. ***On school resources:*** What resources does your school have? Do you have local or international partners? Do you have laboratory equipment or materials whose use you can maximize?

Planning Learning, Teaching, and Assessment using the experiences and outcome key messages:

WHAT TO DO KEY MESSAGES:

• Use long-term plans to outline the structure of the year and the ways in which learning is organized throughout the whole year.

• Keep medium-term planning short and focused on the main learning activities developed from the Experiences and Outcomes (Es and Os). Group Es and Os together in ways that best suit learners.

• Short-term planning on a daily or weekly basis should be flexible and be regarded as working notes to help organize learning.

• Take a collegiate approach to moderation of planning learning, teaching and assessment.

• Work together with colleagues to review and reduce any unnecessary bureaucracy. Plan and organize learning in a way that avoids each week at school feeling too cluttered to provide space and time for depth of learning.

• Planning should include consideration of how best the needs of individuals and groups of children and young people will be met.

• Prioritize literacy, numeracy, and health and wellbeing across the curriculum to ensure that all learners make the best possible progress.

• Plan interdisciplinary learning (IDL) to make natural links across learning. Be aware of what is happening in other subjects and make connections.

• All planning must focus directly on enhancing the learner's journey. When asked to complete paperwork that does not directly relate to improving the learner journey, challenge this with your colleagues.

WHAT TO AVOID

• Avoid writing overly-detailed plans for the year ahead which limit your flexibility to respond to children's and young people's needs, interests and progression.

• Do not plan for individual Es and Os or spend excessive time writing detailed descriptions of learning activities.

• Do not 'tick off' all of the Es and Os separately.

• Do not spend excessive time completing detailed daily or weekly planning templates or writing detailed evaluations of plans.

Avoid unnecessary bureaucracy creeping back in overtime.

• Stop doing too many things at the same time. For example, in a primary school, covering all eight curriculum areas every week.

• Do not lose a clear focus on helping all children and young people to progress at an appropriate pace and achieve the highest standards in literacy, numeracy, and health and wellbeing.

• Do not spend time on IDL which does not provide opportunities to apply and deepen learning or is contrived.

ASSESSMENT USING THE BENCHMARKS:

The purpose of the Benchmarks is to set out very clear statements about what children and young people need to learn to achieve each level of the curriculum. Benchmarks streamline and embed a wide range of existing assessment guidance (significant aspects of learning, progression frameworks, and annotated exemplification) into one key resource to support teachers' professional judgments.

KEY MESSAGES –

WHAT TO DO KEY MESSAGES

• Periodically (from time to time) use assessments to sample and pull together learning in a joined-up way.

• Plan an appropriate balance between ongoing and periodic assessment – this will vary from stage to stage.

• Moderate assessment judgments by taking account of a sample of evidence from different sources to discuss standards and the progress of learners.

• As a school, develop simple and effective approaches to monitoring and tracking learners' progress particularly in literacy and numeracy. Tracking needs to be as easy to use as possible.

Regularly discuss tracking information with colleagues to plan additional support and interventions to help improve learners' progress.

• Evaluate learners' progress on an ongoing basis and keep short concise notes to help plan for the next steps in learning. This will include identifying where additional support and challenge may be needed.

• Use the benchmarks to help monitor progress and support the overall professional judgment of when a learner has achieved a curriculum level.

• Involve children and young people in leading their own learning and involve them in profiling their achievements.

• Reporting to parents should highlight the latest progress, identify the next steps in learning and build on profiling. Discussions should highlight ways in which parents can support their child's progress.

WHAT TO AVOID

• Avoid spending time on assessment activities that do not help to identify children's and young people's next steps in learning.

• Do not over-assess learners or assess the same content repeatedly in different ways. Do not create large portfolios of evidence.

• Avoid duplication and keep evidence of every detail within the Benchmark.

• Avoid waiting until learners have demonstrated evidence of every aspect of learning within the Benchmarks before moving on to the next level.

• Avoid undue pressure on learners with too many assessments in different subjects at once.

• Avoid spending too much time collecting a wide range of evidence for moderation purposes.

• Do not track and record progress against individual Es and Os.

• Do not track progress and achievement using the terms 'developing, consolidating, secure'.

• Do not spend time writing long reports for parents which describe lots of classwork or use professional jargon.

Summary of the Curriculum Framework:

This summary is for teachers and practitioners, including those in early learning and childcare, youth work, and colleges. It provides clarity of the main messages.

CHAPTER V

WHAT SKILLS ARE REQUIRED FOR THE 21ST CENTURY?

The Future of Work and Careers

This brings us to our own time, our recently arrived Knowledge Age. In our new flat world of connected knowledge work, global markets, tele-linked citizens, and blended cultural traditions, the 21st century demands a fresh set of responses.

The study clearly showed that students graduating from secondary schools, technical colleges, and universities are sorely lacking in some basic skills and a large number of applied skills:

1. Oral and written communications.
2. Critical thinking and problem-solving.
3. Professionalism and work ethic.
4. Teamwork and collaboration.
5. Working in diverse teams.
6. Applying technology.
7. Leadership and project management.

Reports from around the world confirm that this "21st-century skills gap" is costing businesses a great deal of money. Some estimate that well over $200 billion a year is spent worldwide in finding and hiring scarce, highly skilled talent, and in bringing new employees up to required skill levels through costly training programs. And as budgets tighten further in tough economic times, companies need highly competent employees ready to hit the ground running without extra training and development costs.

The competitiveness and wealth of corporations and countries are completely dependent on having a well-educated workforce—as

"Learning Is Earning." Improving a country's literacy rate by a small amount can have huge positive economic impacts. Education also increases the earning potential of workers—an additional year of schooling can improve a person's lifetime wages.

Why is education falling short in preparing students for 21ˢᵗ-century work?

The world of Knowledge Age work requires a new mix of skills. Jobs that require routine manual and thinking skills are giving way to jobs that involve higher levels of knowledge and applied skills like expert thinking and complex communication.

The rising demand for a highly-skilled workforce also means that there will be a growing income gap between less educated, relatively unskilled workers and highly educated, highly skilled workers. Routine tasks are increasingly being automated, and the routine jobs are still done by people barely paid a living wage. Routine work is moving to countries where the cost of labor is very low, the shift is visible in many parts of the world.

Our world's education systems must now prepare as many students as possible for jobs at the top of the chart—the high-paying knowledge work jobs of today and tomorrow that require complex skills, expertise, and creativity. And many of the jobs of the future do not even exist today! If all these changes weren't quite enough, students in school today can expect to have more than eleven different jobs between the ages of eighteen and forty-two.[4] We don't know yet how many more job changes to expect after age forty-two, but with increasing life expectancy, the number could easily double to twenty-two or more total jobs in a lifetime.

What is certain is that two essential skill sets will remain at the top of the list of job requirements for 21ˢᵗ-century work.

1. The ability to quickly acquire and apply new knowledge.
2. The know-how to apply essential 21ˢᵗ-century skills problem-solving, communication, teamwork, technology use, innovation,

and the rest—to each and every project, the primary unit of 21st-century work.

To get a better sense of the rising importance learning and education are playing in our lives today, it's useful to step back and take a look at the roles education has played in the past, where learning is heading, and the forces driving these changes.

Learning Through Time Currently,

Nearly 2.0 billion children attend primary and secondary schools in the world—around 77 percent of all school-age children.

A 2.0 billion school children is a staggering number, even though it leaves out another three hundred million and more worldwide—most of the girls—who have no access to basic education.

But why is education so important that virtually every country in the world has implemented some sort of formal education system? Why has the United Nations declared it a fundamental right of all children? And what do parents, teachers, businesses, social institutions, governments, and society as a whole expect from education? Have these expectations changed over time?

Education's Purpose & Framework in the past:

It has been observed that today's education systems operate on an agrarian calendar (summers off to allow students to work in the fields), an industrial time clock (45-minute classroom periods marked by bells), and a list of curriculum subjects invented in the middle ages (language, math, science, and the arts). It's useful to take a brief look at how this came about and what education's role has been in ages past, before turning to what education means for us now and in the future.

- What do a one-room school in a rural farming village, a crowded classroom in a bustling industrial city, and a shiny new school in a high-tech suburban zone have in common?
- What do we expect them to do for our children?
- What have we expected from our schools through time?

Education plays four universal roles in society's evolving stage. It empowers us to contribute to work and society, exercise and develop our personal talents, fulfills our civic responsibilities, and carry our traditions and values forward. These are the "great expectations," the big returns we want from our investments in education. Or put another way, these are the four universal goals we expect the education of our children to achieve.

These four pillars of education's purpose remain constant through time— The world education community entered a new era in which education is expected to contribute not only to the fulfillment of individual and national aspirations, but also to ensure the well-being of all humanity and the global community.

In 2015, **Global Citizenship Education** was included as one of the topic areas of Target 4.7 of the Sustainable Development Goal on Education that countries must promote and address. These two developments provided the impetus for the world community to pay attention to this particular topic area at the policy level.

In the Agrarian Age, when farming the land was the primary work of society (as it still is in many parts of the world), contributing to society meant learning how to grow food for more than your family. Passing on the knowledge, traditions, and crafts of rural life to your children was an essential survival need. Children worked in the fields next to their parents and other family members, and education beyond farming skills was not a high priority. Civic responsibilities revolved around doing what you could to help your neighbors and others in your village when they were in need, as they would in turn help you when you were in need. The social compact was simple and practical.

In the Industrial Age, when the population dramatically shifted from farm to city and work moved from the fields to the factories, education played new roles in society. Typically, men had one or two career paths: working in a trade, factory, or clerical job, or becoming a manager, administrator, or professional if they could make the grade. Women's choices were, of course, far fewer.

The real challenge for industry was to train as many factory and trade workers as possible. So standardization, uniformity, and mass production were important to both the factory and the classroom. Those few destined for managerial or professional work were given special learning opportunities to develop their potential.

Engineering and science skills, the new engines for industrial growth, were particularly prized, along with the management and financial skills necessary to keep the industrial complex running port unities to develop their potential smoothly. And with the great mixing of cultures in urban centers, people became more aware (and eventually more tolerant) of traditions different from their own.

Education's Role in the 21ˢᵗ Century.

In the Knowledge Age, brainpower replaces brawn power, and mechanical horsepower gives way to electronic hertz power. Achieving education's goals in our times is shaped by the increasingly powerful technologies we have for communicating, collaborating, and learning. And learning assumes a central role throughout life.

Contributing to Work and Society:

To be a productive contributor to society in our 21ˢᵗ century, you need to be able to quickly learn the core content of a field of knowledge while also mastering a broad portfolio of essential learning, innovation, technology, and career skills needed for work and life. And when you apply these skills to today's knowledge and innovation work, you are participating in a global network in which, for example, a product may be designed in California, manufactured in China, assembled in the Czech Republic, and sold in chain stores in cities across the world.

This global network of economic, technological, political, social, and ecological interconnections is no less than breathtaking. We work with the support of multiple teams spread across the world to get things done, solve problems, and create and deliver new services. But since our interlinked economies depend on both natural and human resources from around the globe, we must continually find new ways to preserve our natural world while building more harmonious, culturally rich, and creative societies.

Today nearly two billion cell phones are in use around the world, and access to the Internet is rapidly increasing in schools, homes, community centers, and Internet cafés worldwide. This is providing even more opportunities to learn and develop skills.

As amplifiers, storerooms, and sensory extensions for our thinking and communicating, digital devices and the Internet are today's power tools for building abilities and sharing talents. Making these tools universally accessible and closing the digital divide between the information-rich and the information poor will provide more opportunities for learners to realize their potential. People everywhere will then be able to contribute their own special talents and gifts to the health and welfare of their community, the economy, and society as a whole.

Fulfilling Civic Responsibilities

With access to the expanded spectrum of issues, facts, opinions, and conversations that our increasingly media-rich and Internet-connected world brings us, our potential for informed participation in democratic decision-making has never been better. E-mail, the Internet, and cell phones have made it easier to connect with others who share our interests and concerns and to coordinate our social, civic, and community activities.

At the same time, the potential for information overload, distraction, and analysis paralysis when facing demands for attention from too many sources—ranging from well-informed and reliable to woefully uninformed and even deliberately misleading—is also high. Learning to manage our digital power tools and to apply the critical thinking and information literacy skills needed to put all this information to good use is a clear challenge for the 21st century.

In many ways, we are just beginning to understand how to tap the enormous power of online social technologies for collaborative problem solving, political action, and community building.

Carrying Forward Traditions and Values Learning

The core principles and traditions of a field of knowledge and blending these with the knowledge and practices of other fields to invent and introduce new knowledge, new services, and new products, will be a high-demand skill set in the 21st century.

Increased mobility, immigration, intermarriage, and access to job opportunities worldwide have led to another kind of blending and mixing—communities across the globe are becoming ever more culturally diverse. Though this diversity has brought vitality and richness to our communities, differences between traditional culture and modern values are still a troubling source of tension in the world.

The 21st-century challenge for each of us is to build and maintain our own identity from our given traditions and from the wide variety of traditions all around us. At the same time, we must all learn to apply tolerance and compassion for the different identities and values of others.

Our historic shift to a 21st century Knowledge Age, decades in the making, has forever tilted the balance of what is needed and valued in our work, our learning, and our life. In the 21st century, lifelong learning is here to stay.

CHAPTER VI

WHAT WILL BE THE NEW NORM OF THE SCHOOLING SYSTEM? (ONLINE AND TECHNOLOGY BASED & OFFLINE PRACTICAL BASED.)

The advancement of technology and its use for sustainability.

Phenomenal advances in information and communication technologies (ICTs) have enabled people to connect and interact with others around the world anywhere, anytime. This has contributed to an intensified perception and reality of being interconnected and living beyond local perimeters. Moreover, increased transnational migration is making local communities inevitably more heterogeneous, increasing the need to learn how to live together.

Tensions and conflicts among populations that have causes and impacts beyond national boundaries, and challenges for sustainable development, including climate change, also call for cooperation and collective actions at both global and local levels.

The pandemic has disturbed all sectors of society and revealed its fault lines—especially in our education systems. The reaction to the crisis has generated some impressive responses on the part of individuals and small groups as educators have stepped up to serve their communities. In some cases, public and private partnerships have filled the gaps. Some systems have been able to rapidly deliver remote learning experiences, but most have struggled with meeting the needs of all. Equity, access, and capacity left wanting. Prior to the pandemic, many education systems were stalled, the pandemic exposed the case that fundamental changes are needed.

Through this disruption, there has been recognition that schools play a vital role beyond learning. Their custodial and community roles are central to a healthy society. As we grapple with the issues of reopening schools in this uncertain time, we must seize the opportunity to reflect on what has been learned, and what matters most.

The challenges highlighted during the disruption should not come as a surprise. Over the last decade, student engagement has plummeted. 1 Almost one in every five students does not reach a basic minimum level of skills to function in today's society (OECD) Moreover, many school systems have not maintained pace with technological advances; schools have not provided widespread access to digital tools. When the pandemic hit, 1 in 5 students did not have access to the internet or a device to support them in lockdown. This disruption revealed systems that already struggled to support all learners. To put it plainly: it's time to situate education as an instrument of individual and societal good.

How will we choose to respond? Will we patch together a reaction, or use this opportunity to transform the system itself? The question becomes, what will be more appealing - reverting to the status quo or using the opportunity to help students become knowledgeable and skilled change-makers through deeper learning? We argue that the solutions lie before us. We have the opportunity to creatively manage the immediate issues while building a bridge to a re-imagined education system.

Reimagining education in the 21ˢᵗ century:

We must lay out a vision for an educational approach that enables all students to thrive and prepares them with skills to navigate ambiguity and change in the 21ˢᵗ century. This phase draws from the best of **traditional approaches, innovative practices, and insights from remote learning to shape new, flexible, agile hybrid deep learning models.**

The new approaches would enable well-being, equity, and quality (deep) learning to flourish. In order to realize such improvement, it is imperative to embrace an innovative mindset.

We will need to be open to rethinking and creating a powerful new future that meets everyone's needs.

Not everyone or every system had the same experience in facing this abrupt change. Some systems had stronger collaboration and technology infrastructure which assisted them in a more rapid response while others were struggling to find the right pathway.

Disruptions in PANDEMIC:

At the pandemic's peak, 1.6 billion students were out of school in the world. This move was abrupt and unprecedented, leaving policymakers and practitioners scrambling to provide a safe and expedient way to provide learning at home. Remote learning became the quick fix. The lack of access and connectivity meant that students would be denied schooling for months of shut down.

According to PISA, slightly more than two-thirds of 15-year-old students in OECD countries were enrolled in schools where digital devices had sufficient computing capacity. And on average, not even half of 15-year-olds were in schools with an effective online learning support platform. In those schools, most principals considered their teachers to have the necessary technical and pedagogical skills to integrate digital devices in instruction.

Some systems with experience in designing and delivering online learning made the transition to remote learning with limited disruption. Many worked quickly to provide lessons via tv, radio, or by making available paper-based packets of learning materials. The technology and communications sectors rapidly reprioritized and provided support to the education sector; some districts redirected resources to acquire and distribute devices, especially to those who needed them. In some cases, mobile buses circled through needy neighborhoods to provide Wi-Fi to students who lacked connectivity.

Besides, from the widespread technological deficits that hampered learning for all, this period also revealed that digital alone could not replace the social and pedagogical impact of teachers. Parents recognized that the craft of teaching is not as simple as it appears. Teachers also play a vital role as relationship builders and connectors. In response, teachers embraced technology to reach out to students and families.

Important new requirement for Education in the Pandemic:

A framework to guide an education response to the COVID-19 Pandemic of 2020 which includes responses from 98 countries. The report reveals some of the priority considerations and responses made as systems sought to build a 'new normal.

- The issues identified as very challenging by most respondents were:
- Ensuring the continuity of academic learning for students.

1. Supporting the students who lack skills for independent study.
2. Ensuring continuity and integrity of the assessment of student learning.
3. Ensuring support for parents so they can support student learning.
4. Ensuring the well-being of students and of teachers.

There are numerous barriers to the implementation. Educators and policymakers recognized that these issues would not be easily resolved

Barriers included:

1. Availability of technological infrastructure.
2. Addressing student emotional well-being.
3. Addressing the right balance between digital and screen-free activities.
4. Managing the technological infrastructure.

The COVID crisis elevated the importance of digital. However, the most agile schools and districts have been able to move beyond simply elevated digital importance, to elevated impact. In Hong Kong, the English Schools Foundation (ESF) had a strong technology platform. Their learning, as they moved through the disruption, was that the quality of learning was not dependent on digital being the medium but on "HOW" the use of digital shifted from a simple delivery system to a robust mechanism for culture building and social connectedness.

It becomes clear that technology is a crucial part of the solution during the disruption. What emerges is a recognition, that it is time to move beyond a blend of traditional teaching & online instruction, both happening within brick & mortar, and to something more, which is called <u>Integrative Blended Learning</u> through Core Schooling Methods.

Key Learning of the Teachers and Leaders in the field of Education:

Teachers and leaders who were able to move through the corvid-19 phase reported some important learning.

What they discovered was so powerful that they did not want to slip back to the status quo:

1. Acknowledgment that well-being was a critical pre-condition for learning.
2. Technology shifted from being a vehicle for delivery/ transmission to a mechanism for collaboration, social connectedness, and culture building.
3. Self-regulation and learning to learn were key determinants of student motivation, engagement, and success.
4. Students who found themselves with more choice and voice exceeded expectations finding ways to help themselves and collaborate with others.

5. Collaboration among teachers and leaders emerged because the focus was clear.
6. In the absence of high-stakes testing, systems relied on teacher and leader's professional judgments.

Those who took the time to reflect on what was learned about equity, well-being, and learning, began to innovate and see the transition to reopening as a bridge to revitalizing education. Much noted technology was a critical enabler for learning during the Disruption phase and should also play a crucial role in moving towards quality learning in a hybrid model.

The group of students who were affected the most during the pandemic?

Subgroups such as Vulnerable students, Migrant students, Special needs students. It is recommended that beyond identifying those groups, you push to understand why they are vulnerable. Asking "why" illuminates a range of different causes, including deficiencies within our own systems. Only when we understand our deficiencies, can we begin to transform them.

Here are some more examples: •

- **WHY?** It is found that 30% of senior students did not log on. The issue may have been equity as they may not have had access to digital tools or connectivity, or it may be well being was the determinant as they did not have the basic necessities of life.
- **Solutions:** The equity lens may lead to support structures of connectivity and devices, but the well-being lens will require social services. •
- **WHY?** It is found that 55% of students with identified special needs did not complete the work. We might focus on the quality of learning impacting engagement or the lack of independent

learning skills or confidence.

- **Solutions:** They were not engaged we may be led to consider the content chunking, the learning design, or the support structures that were not in place.

There may be a tendency to overlook the learning agenda and become preoccupied with health and safety. We do this at our peril. It is essential to consider ways to improve learning early in the Transition Phase. Before focusing on delivering content, there are a number of considerations that should be made to enable and enhance learning during this Transition time.

Teachers can play a vital role in the student's learning curve:

1. Facilitating connection and conversation.
2. Re-creating norms that will allow students to feel psychologically safe in an optimistic and efficacious learning environment.
3. Inviting each student's perspective by asking open questions so that each student feels connected to the learning community.
4. Providing trauma-informed learning for staff, parents, and students, enabling everyone in the school community to recognize and respond mindfully during this crisis.
5. Appoint a caring adult to build a relationship with those students you know to be vulnerable.

Many may have learning gaps and others will have emerging stressors that will affect their ability to engage cognitively. Still, others may have grown in ways we could not have foreseen. Assessment practices that prioritize emotional well-being are what is needed.

Also, consider that for several months many students have enjoyed autonomy at home. Many have had the latitude to choose when to learn, when to move around and how to manage their own time. Some have pursued their own interests through play. Others have chosen to opt-out of learning entirely. Educators would be wise to examine their own practices that can extend flexibility, choice, and voice to students.

Use of technology and new learning methods:

Even before the pandemic, there was readiness building for a new system of learning. The current system had stalled, and the pandemic vividly exposed our systemic inability to optimize the use of technology, and truly ensure equity, well-being, and quality of learning.

Education reform has been high on the agenda for many systems but has focused narrowly on literacy, numeracy, and high school graduation without addressing the holistic needs of students in an increasingly unpredictable global society. Quality learning must be built on the interests of students along the following dimensions.

- Connecting to purpose and meaning.
- Challenging students to have high expectations.
- Positioning learning goals that focus beyond the basics.
- Using engaging pedagogies.
- Building relationships and belongingness.

Providing opportunities to contribute to the world We see glimpses of this potentially powerful reform across the globe and indeed some strong examples in our global network: New Pedagogies for Deep Learning (NPDL). This combination of readiness for change and urgency arising from the current crisis has the potential to shift the education system from one of outdated "schooling" to future-focused 'learning" and take learning out of the classroom and into the world.

Reflect and Re-imagine Education: This pandemic has magnified the question of what kind of learning is required in the

21st Century and beyond. To re-imagine learning we need to reflect on what we know about learning, our students, the new role of technology, and the complexity of an unknown future. Six key questions can foster deep reflection and be used to engage all who need to be part of the solution- students, parents and families, educators, and community partners. What is crucial is to take this opportunity to ask the tough questions of your system, discuss possibilities and take action for a new and better future.

1. What knowledge, skills, and attributes do our students need to thrive in the fast-changing technology and AI applications in the 21st Century?

2. What kind of learning is needed for this current and future complexity?

3. How do we ensure equity?

4. How do we attend to well-being?

5. What have we learned from remote learning?

6. How can technology be best leveraged for learning in the future?

The prevailing model of schooling was built on two organizing (and confining) constructs time (when kids learned) and space (where they learned). These two constructs were useful in the 1800 and 1900s but the COVID disruption has rendered them redundant. Students can learn and demonstrate this learning without bricks and mortar or bell times. With digital and deep learning, students can learn where they are. Students can learn when they are ready.

Students who thrived in the remote environment during the pandemic demonstrated competencies such as critical thinking, creativity, resilience, independence as learners, self-regulation, cognitive flexibility, and perseverance. These are the attributes that are noted as critical for future employability across industries and geographies.9 Going forward the learning process must foster these competencies through authentic, relevant learning that provides voice, choice, and agency to learners. This necessitates a new role for teachers; one in which they are activators of learning; practitioners who can differentiate task, time, and space to meet student needs and include them as co-designers of that learning. The challenge is to integrate the best of what we have learned from this remote phase with the new skill set required for the future.

Disruption has triggered the potential energy for change that has not seen any action in many systems. What is now needed is a model that integrates the best of remote-learning and school situated learning, a new hybrid model.

Deep Learning experiences Are those that produce learning that sticks for life. They are both profoundly personalized and students centered and are intrinsically motivating for students as they pursue topics that are of real interest to them, have authentic meaning, and are more rigorous. These learning experiences make students want to persist and succeed. This combination of autonomy, belonging, and meaningful work inspires students.

Deep Learning provides the foundation for a new hybrid learning environment: This new hybrid model fosters the best of remote and in-school learning and facilitates the shift to a learner-centered model. Studies suggest12 that combining face-to-face and remote learning may be as effective as classroom learning when important design factors include engaging content, opportunities for interaction with teachers and peers, and support for learners.

We know that peer interaction is important for learning and have seen the power of collaborative platforms to connect students across time and space. Connectedness and belonging can be supported through emotional check-ins built into digital learning environments. Engagement is a key determinant of learning and can be amplified through Virtual Real-Life experiences; museum and gallery tours, simulations, and sandbox environments where students explore and create across time and space with experts and partners. Artificial Intelligence can offer translation, transcription, presentation, feedback, and peer and self-assessment tools.

CHAPTER VII

UNESCO – GECD AND SDG PRINCIPLES & TEACHERS IMPACTING STUDENTS LEARNING IN THE 21ST CENTURY

Roll of Teachers

Teachers play a critical role in education. Besides transferring knowledge content to learners, teachers are expected to create an environment that is conducive to learning and to prepare their students to be productive, ethical, moral, and responsible citizens in a rapidly changing and interconnected world. To do so, we want our teachers to have strong subject and pedagogic content knowledge, possess effective classroom management skills, readily adopt new technologies, and be inclusive and sensitive to the diverse needs of their students. Our demands are high and so are the stakes: the quality of an education system cannot exceed the quality of its teachers and the quality of teaching. Therefore, building the capacity of teachers to meet the challenges is a top priority.

To demonstrate how creative pedagogies can be practically applied, the following section presents some examples: P.E.A.C.E., Flipped Classroom, Event-based Learning, Storytelling, Using Threshold Concepts, Bricolage, Facilitation as Transformative Pedagogy, Arts-based Inquiry Pedagogy, Design Thinking, and Project-based Learning. These pedagogies are not meant to be used in isolation since there are many overlapping philosophies and similarities. Rather, it is useful to show how different types of teaching methods and tools can be combined to match the learning objectives and outcomes, utilizing ICT to optimize the learning experiences where necessary.

Flipped classroom

Flipped learning reverses the traditional classroom approach to teaching and learning. It moves direct instruction into the learner's own space. At home or during individual study time in school, students watch inputs such as video lectures that offer them opportunities to work at their own pace, pausing to make notes where necessary. This allows time in class to be spent on activities that exercise critical thinking, with the teacher guiding students in creative exploration of the topics they are studying. It also offers opportunities for the classroom to become a more flexible environment where the physical layout can be shifted to enable group work, where students can make use of their own devices, and where new approaches to learning and assessment are put into practice (Sharples et al., 2014).

Essentially, the flipped classroom technique turns a didactic class into a process or environment for knowledge building. With students' prior learning before the class, students can share their initial learning experiences that can be conglomerated into structured knowledge, as facilitated by the teacher. The teacher may add the following pedagogies to improve the learning: Dialogical Relationship in a Learning Community, Writing Pre-Post Narrative Inquiries, Engagement, and Reflection on Activities, Critical

Textual Discourse, Engagement in Structured and Threaded Discussions, Experiencing Humanizing Pedagogy (Ukpokodu, 2009).

Event-based Learning

Event-based learning runs over a few hours or days and seeks to create a memorable sense of occasion for learners engaged in it. Examples are the "maker fairs" that gather together enthusiasts who are keen on do-it-yourself science, engineering, and crafts projects, and the "Raspberry jams" where fans of the Raspberry Pi computer meet up and share ideas. Local events can spark national gatherings and these can build into international festivals. The time-bounded nature of an event encourages people to learn together; its local settings support face-to-face encounters between amateurs and experts, and the scale of an event ca participants. Having such an event as a focus gives learners something concrete to work towards and to reflect upon afterward, together with a sense of personal engagement and excitement (Sharples et al., 2014).

Storytelling:

Learning requires a structure that helps learners to embed and revisit their understanding.

Stories provide one way of creating this structure. Developing a narrative is part of a process in which the narrator structures a series of events from a particular point of view in order to create a meaningful whole. Writing up an experiment, reporting on an inquiry, analyzing a period of history – these are all examples of narrative supporting learning. Indeed, much of our education involves combining different things we know in order to create an understanding of what has happened and, as a consequence, what can be expected to happen in the future. These accounts can be used to link memories of events, binding them together to form larger, more coherent chunks.

In a narrative approach to learning, the creation of stories is emphasized, allowing learners to navigate resources and to add coherence to different experiences. Narrative encourages the combination of historical overview and modern practice. It can provide emotional engagement and relevance for learners, together with personal involvement and immersion (Sharples et al., 2014).

Using threshold concepts

A threshold concept is something that, when learned, opens up a new way of thinking about a problem, a subject, or the world. An example is the physics concept of heat transfer that can inform everyday activities such as cooking or home energy use. These concepts help to define subjects, they shift learners' perceptions of a topic area, and they usually prove difficult to unlearn. Teachers are increasingly using threshold concepts as starting points for the design of effective lessons. They can also be used as a focus for dialogue between students, teachers, and educational designers. A challenging aspect of threshold concepts is that they often seem strange unintuitive or counterintuitive. Students who appear to have understood these troublesome concepts may be unable to put them into practice, instead of falling back on common-sense but inaccurate beliefs. Momentum for using threshold concepts to help to teach is growing across disciplines. One approach is to develop standard sets of threshold concepts for different subject areas; another is to embed them in teaching and learning processes and practices (Sharples et al., 2014).

Bricolage

Bricolage is a practical process of learning through tinkering with materials. It involves continual transformation, with earlier products or materials that are ready to become resources for new constructions. It is a fundamental process of children's learning through play as they create castles out of boxes and tell stories from remembered events. It also forms a basis for creative innovation, allowing inventors to combine and adapt tools and theories to generate new insights, while also engaging with relevant communities to ensure that the innovation works in practice and in context (Sharples et al., 2014).

Arts-based Inquiry as Pedagogy

Arts-based pedagogy or arts inquiry is a student-centered approach that connects cognitive learning experiences to emotive ones. Learners are enabled to examine their assumptions, understanding, and beliefs by viewing different perspectives through experimentation, development, and expression of self-esteem, identity, voice, compassion, and empathy. It is highly suited for integrated studies across the curriculum to include the various forms of art: Dance, Drama, Media, Music, and Visual Art. Learning is based on questions and discussions linking the artworks to ethics, culture, and socio-political issues, for example. As part of the process, students create artworks to demonstrate their experiences and knowledge, either individually or in groups and present them to an audience for further discussions and learning. Higher-order thinking skills can be acquired such as active engagement in linking abstract concepts to the Arts (Power, 2014).

Design Thinking

Design Thinking is a human-centered approach to finding and solving problems that can be applied in different contexts. Widely used in business and education settings today, and relies on a constant stream of feedback. It operates under the idea that the process of making products and services should be fluid and must be flexible enough to adapt to real-life situations. It has been used across a wide range of disciplines for years, so there is a copious amount and rich variety of resources freely available online to frame the users' conceptual understanding of design thinking as a pedagogical tool to teach GCED (IDEO, 2012; Wyatt, n.d.; Habi Education Lab. n.d.; Institute of Design at Stanford, n.d.).

Design Thinking can be used by teachers to encourage students to be active global citizens focused on solving real-life problems. Each step of the Design Thinking framework – (Empathize – Define – Ideate – Prototype – Test) – has a specific goal, and the users must go through the full cycle to maximize the entire process. Initially, teachers may begin by deconstructing the process and centering their efforts on one or two steps.

Project-based Learning

Project-based Learning (PBL) is defined as a student-centered approach where students actively engage in a curriculum-based project driven by authentic real-world problems that often require expert-like thinking. In PBL, students typically work in teams to achieve commonly defined and measurable learning goals. Students work on actual products as project outputs that are targeted for a certain audience, thus extending the impact of student learning beyond classrooms. A teacher or a group of teachers facilitates the student learning process and reflection throughout the four steps of PBL activities.

The Global Education First Initiative (GEFI) has identified the lack of teacher's capacity at a GCED. As key actors in ensuring quality education, teachers face a lot of pressure. They are required to deepen their knowledge base and pedagogic skills in response to new demands and changing curricula. Effective teaching needs practice and teachers must be nurtured through high-quality training and continuous. Learning programs to ensure that they are equipped with the necessary knowledge and skills to do their job well.

The UNESCO Asia-Pacific Regional Bureau for Education in Bangkok, Thailand, has a project in place to enhance the capacity of teachers to transmit appropriate and relevant knowledge and skills about global citizenship to their students. A key output of the project– Preparing Teachers for Global Citizenship Education: A Template. Ultimately, the project seeks to empower learners, through their teachers, to engage and assume active roles in addressing and resolving local and global challenges.

The 2016 Global Education Monitoring Report highlighted a shortage of information about how teachers are trained in areas related to global citizenship, including empathy, understanding discrimination, cultural sensitivity, tolerance, acceptance, and communication skills in 10 countries in Asia and the Pacific (UNESCO, 2017a). Evidently, more has to be done to fill the gap in pre-service teacher education as well as in-service professional development.

The Whole Schools Approach for GCED

There is no doubt that the efforts of individual teachers are critical for implementing GCED; however, having the support of the entire school system is more likely to make a longer-lasting impact on learners. The whole school approach has been used to promote education in many areas: health, human rights, inclusion, tolerance environment, sustainability, and so on. A whole-school approach "means carrying out work in different spaces across the school – including within the curriculum, extra-curricular activities, teacher training, and engaging the community. It also means doing this in a coordinated way that links to an overarching vision or purpose for your global citizenship work. Working holistically in this way will have more impact on young people, increasing the benefits for them as individuals, as learners, and as future citizens. It can also have additional benefits for the school, supporting curriculum development, pupil motivation, and staff" as a whole school approach to climate change that includes action in every aspect of school life (school governance, teaching content and methodology) and facilities management and with the community partnerships. It involves all school-related stakeholders: students, teachers, principals, school staff at all levels, families, and community members. Examples of whole-school programs around the world that highlight the effective integration of the learning objectives into all parts of school life in the emerging area of anti-bullying education. To prevent and reduce bullying, a combination of broad strategies can include the following:

1. Increase awareness of bullying through school assemblies;
2. Encourage student-planned activities;
3. Practice effective classroom rules and management;
4. Promote a positive school environment, relationships, and student well-being;

5. Apply effective methods of behavior management that are non-hostile and non-punitive;
6. Provide skill development for all students, and especially bystanders;
7. Stand against bullying behavior and support students who are bullied.

Given the benefits of a whole school approach and its holistic perspective on educational transformation, it is not surprising that the whole school approach for GCED has the support of many advocates.

Education for International Understanding

Human Rights Education

Education and Training, based on principles of equality, states that human rights education and training include all education, training, information, awareness-raising, and learning activities aimed at promoting universal respect for and observance of human rights and fundamental freedoms. Human rights is a lifelong process that increases people's knowledge, skills, and understanding, develops their attitudes and behavior, and empowers them to contribute to the building and promotion of a universal culture of human rights.

Development Education

Most newly independent countries (developing or global South nations) adopted national development policies with the aid of developed or global North countries and various intergovernmental or international agencies. These policies promised economic growth, foreign investments, and the alleviation of poverty. However, many international and local non-governmental organizations (NGOs) noted that the outcomes of such development strategies premised on unequal world order tended to increase social and economic injustices within and across nations. As a result, the field of Development Education, or Education for Local/Global Justice, emerged with the aim of facilitating marginalized peoples in global South contexts to better understand the root causes of their situation and organize for alternative development initiatives that meet their rights and overcome their marginalization, while concerned people in global North societies are catalyzed to help build a just world.

Intercultural and Multicultural Education

The increasing rural-urban and cross-border migrations of people who come from diverse cultures and ethnic groups, speak different languages, and practice different religions and social norms have led to today's multicultural societies. The concept of interculturality refers to evolving relations between cultural groups, while multiculturality describes the culturally diverse nature of human society. To foster harmonious and respectful relationships among learners, Intercultural Education provides them with the cultural knowledge, attitudes, and skills necessary to achieve active and comprehensive participation in society, and enable them to contribute to increased respect, understanding, and solidarity among individuals, as well as ethnic, social, cultural and religious groups and nations (UNESCO, 2006). Multicultural Education seeks to foster and preserve cultural diversity; promote the understanding of unique cultural and ethnic heritages; facilitate the development of culturally responsible and responsive curricula; aid in the acquisition of the attitudes, skills, and knowledge to function in various cultures; eliminate racism and discrimination in society; and achieve social, political, economic, and educational equity. Variations in this field include Antiracist Education, which emphasizes the need to overcome structural, systemic, or institutional racism and racial discrimination; Indigenous Education, which advocates the integration of indigenous knowledge, values, and spiritual traditions in educational systems vital to the cultural social survival of indigenous peoples; and Education for Interfaith Dialogue, which seeks to promote understanding and respect among members of diverse faiths and religions who can then cooperate better to build a peaceful, just and sustainable world based on shared and common values and principles.

Peace Education or Education for a Culture of Peace

Reflecting a long history of educational thought and practice based on the formation of l with other peoples, Peace Education intersects with many other fields of transformative

education. It promotes a critical understanding of the root causes of conflicts, violence, and discord in the world across the full diversity of issues and problems and from macro to micro levels of life; simultaneously it develops an empowered commitment to values, attitudes, and skills for individual and societal actions to transform selves, families, communities, institutions, nations and the world from a culture of war, violence, and discord to a culture of peace and active non-violence.

Values Education

Affirming that human beings and their cultures or civilizations are integrally shaped by their values and principles, Values Education was developed as a process of teaching and learning about the ideals that society deems important. The underlying aim is for students not only to understand the values but also to reflect them in their attitudes and behavior with the aim of contributing to society through good citizenship and ethical practice (DeNobile and Hogan, 2014). Most importantly, Values Education should not merely be a mechanistic transmission of "national values" to passive learners; rather, it is an active learning process whereby students engage in a critical understanding of values and their implications for ethical and responsible personal and social conduct and institutional transformation (Turnbull, 2002).

Education for the Four Pillars of Learning

The Report to UNESCO of the International Commission on Education for the 21st Century, entitled Learning: The Treasure Within, conceptualized the four pillars of learning as **Learning to Know, Learning to Do, Learning to Be and learning to Live together** (UNESCO, n.d.b; Delors et al., 1998). It is worthwhile to note that "learning to live together" refers to the interaction and relatedness of human beings and is the essence of citizenship education.

Citizenship Education

Worldwide, national educational systems have sought to promote the goal of developing responsible citizens who will contribute to the well-being of their nations. Citizenship Education has three main objectives: educating people in citizenship and human rights through an understanding of the principles and institutions (which govern a state or nation); learning to exercise one's judgment and critical faculty, and acquiring a sense of individual and community responsibilities. It emphasizes the importance of educating children, from early childhood, to become clear-thinking and enlightened citizens who participate in decisions concerning society. One more specific framework of citizenship education is civic education, which seeks to teach the knowledge, skills, and values regarded as necessary for democratic institutions.

Education for Gender Equality

Catalyzed by the world conferences on women since the mid-1970s as well as human rights movements, inter-governmental and international agencies, and many governments have pledged to resolve the serious problem of gender inequalities worldwide. Education for Gender Equality seeks to remove gender disparities in access to schooling, address systemic barriers faced especially by girls and women, develop gender-sensitive curriculum and pedagogy, overcome gender-based violence in educational, social, and cultural institutions, and empower girls and women to fulfill their full potentials and become equal citizens with boys and men.

Global Education

Interrelated with diverse fields of transformative education, notably Peace Education, Multicultural Education, Human Rights Education and Education for Sustainable

Development, Global Education enables people to understand the links between their own lives and those of people throughout the world; increases understanding of the economic, cultural, political, and environmental influences which shape our lives; develops the skills, attitudes, and values which enable people to work together to bring about change and take control of their own lives; and works towards achieving a more just and sustainable world in which power and resources are more equitably shared.

Education for Sustainable Development

Education for Sustainable Development (ESD) emphasizes the urgent need to educate young and adult citizens to commit themselves to the building of sustainable futures or address present and future global challenges and create more sustainable and resilient societies; it empowers learners to make informed decisions and responsible actions for environmental integrity, economic viability and just society for present and future generations, while respecting cultural diversity. ESD motivates learners and citizens of all ages to undertake personal and social actions to eliminate pollution, conserve biodiversity, respond effectively to natural disasters and other emergencies, maintain sustainable lifestyles, and address the crisis of climate change.

Education for 21ˢᵗ Century Skills and Competencies:

The global shift towards knowledge-based economies has led policymakers, employers, and educators to stress the importance of Education for 21ˢᵗ Century Skills and Competencies, i.e. those "skills and competencies young people will be required to have in order to be effective workers and citizens in the knowledge society of the 21ˢᵗ century". These include new skills for accessing, evaluating, and organizing information in digital environments; engaging in research and problem solving; creating new knowledge; enhancing the ability to communicate, exchange, criticize, and present information and ideas, including the use of Information and Communication Technology (ICT) applications; and promote ethical practice and social responsibility.

Education for Preventing Violent Extremism

One of the more recent newcomers to transformative education, Education for Preventing Violent Extremism promotes programs that help build learners' resilience to violent extremism and mitigate the drivers of the phenomena. It seeks to strengthen the capacities of national education systems to appropriately and effectively contribute to national prevention efforts by equipping learners of all ages with the knowledge, values, attitudes, and behaviors that foster responsible global citizenship, critical thinking, empathy, and the ability to take action against violent extremism.

Education for Digital Citizenship

UNESCO has defined digital citizenship as "being able to find, access, use and create information effectively; engage with other users and with content in an active, critical, sensitive and ethical manner; and navigate the online and ICT environment safely and responsibly, while being aware of one's own rights" (UNESCO, 2016a). Hence education for digital citizenship includes the development of basic ICT literacy skills, the empowering of children to be active participants in the digital world, the supporting of teachers to be active advocates for cyber wellness, and the assisting of adults to be mediators of children's ICT use.

Conclusion:

It is clear that substantial efforts have been made to develop and promote diverse transformative education towards a culture of inclusion, equality, and peace. While each field has its own focus, there is considerable overlap in the visions, ideas, concepts, and pedagogical strategies.

What is Global Citizenship Education?

The power of education has no boundaries. It is not enough that we only learn to read, write and count. Through education, we also need to gain knowledge and skills to enhance our lives and benefit our environment. At the same time, we cannot overlook the role of education in inculcating non-cognitive learning outcomes such as values, ethics, social responsibility, civic engagement, and citizenship. Education can transform the way we think and act to build more just, peaceful, tolerant, and inclusive societies.

Against the backdrop of an increasingly globalized and interconnected world and amidst calls for education to promote peace, well-being, prosperity, and sustainability, there is growing interest in Global Citizenship Education (GCED), especially after the launch of the

Global Education First Initiative (GEFI) in 2012, highlighting the role of education in developing values, soft skills, and attitudes for social transformation, GCED strives to foster the following attributes in learners.

1. An attitude supported by an understanding of multiple levels of identity, and the potential for a 'collective identity that transcends individual cultural, religious, ethnic, or other differences;
2. Deep knowledge of global issues and universal values such as justice, equality, dignity, and respect;
3. Cognitive skills to think critically, systemically, and creatively, which includes adopting a multi-perspective approach that recognizes the different dimensions, perspectives, and angles of issues;
4. Non-cognitive skills including social skills such as empathy and conflict resolution, communication skills and aptitudes for networking and interacting with people of different backgrounds, origins, cultures, and perspectives; and
5. Behavioral capacities to act collaboratively and responsibly to find global solutions for global challenges and to strive for the collective good.

The important role of GCED was reaffirmed in the vision of the Education 2030 declared at the World Education Forum 2015, which was co-organized by UNESCO, UNICEF, World Bank, UNDP, UN Women, and the UNHCR in Incheon, the Republic of Korea. The Incheon

Declaration on Education 2030, towards inclusive and equitable quality education and lifelong learning, emphasized that albeit foundational literacy, numeracy, and technological skills are essential.

Lastly, education should not be reduced to anything more than the creation of skilled workers. Rather, quality education must also develop the skills, values, and attitudes that enable citizens to lead healthy and fulfilled lives, make informed decisions, and respond to local and global challenges through education for sustainable development and global citizenship education, as well as human rights education and training in order to achieve the United Nations Education.

Key Principles of GCED

The ABCs of Global Citizenship Education noted that there is no globally agreed definition of global citizenship. Nonetheless, there is sufficient consensus on the key principles. For example, global citizenship has no obligatory legal status. Rather, it refers to a sense of belonging to the global community, a common sense of humanity, and thereby a sense of community towards global well-being.

Global citizenship responsibilities apply to everyone – young and old; rich and poor; national, permanent, and temporary residents. It stresses the political, economic, social, cultural, and environmental inter-dependency and inter-connectedness between the local, national and global arenas.

Essentially, GCED addresses three core conceptual dimensions of learning for education to be transformative, knowledge (cognitive domain) must touch the heart (socio-emotional domain) and turn into action to bring about positive change (behavioral domain). This framework emphasizes an education that fulfills individual and national aspirations and thus ensures the well-being of all humanity and the global community at large.

The Significance and Relevance of GCED

We are living in an increasingly connected and complex world. Science and Technology have accelerated the rate of industrialization, urbanization, and globalization, with expanding networks and channels of communication and transportation connecting people across borders and cultures. We have benefitted from economic, social, and technological advances as measured by the Human Development Index. At the same time, persistent hunger, malnutrition, child mortality, and lack of basic services still affect a majority of the world's population. Using data from several sources, the 2016 Human Development Report presents a somber picture of the challenges we face in order to ensure sustainability, inclusion. and decent work for all the 7.8 billion people who currently inhabit the planet.

The movement of millions of migrants and refugees from one country or region to another – voluntarily or otherwise – has led to the formation of "multicultural" communities. With more than 244 million people living outside their home countries (United Nations, 2016a), social cohesion, mutual respect, and tolerance of differences are critical to overcoming prejudices, ethnocentrism, racism, xenophobia, nationalism, discrimination, and violence. No less important is the continuing marginalization and displacement of indigenous peoples who are facing their own challenges to preserve their traditions, cultures, religions, and practices along the road to economic development. The 2030 Agenda for Sustainable Development, adopted by 193 United Nations Member States in 2015, lays out an ambitious plan of action for people and the planet on the way to universal prosperity on sustainable levels.

To achieve this grand vision, the 2030 Agenda's 17 Sustainable Development Goals (SDGs) seek to eradicate extreme poverty and strengthen universal peace by integrating and balancing the three dimensions of sustainable development – economic, social and environmental–comprehensively. Whereas all the 17 SDGs are important to realize the 2030 Agenda's transformative vision, education is the main driver of development. Education is also implicitly linked to the other SDGs based on the principles of human rights and dignity; social justice; inclusion; protection; cultural, linguistic, and ethnic diversity; and shared responsibility and accountability. SDG 4.0-Education 2030 with 7 outcome targets and 3 means of implementation aims to ensure inclusive and equitable quality education and promote lifelong learning opportunities for all.

By 2030, ensure that all learners acquire the knowledge and skills needed to promote sustainable development, including, among others, through education for sustainable development and sustainable lifestyles, human rights, gender equality, promotion of a culture of peace and nonviolence, global citizenship, and appreciation of cultural diversity and of culture's contribution to sustainable development.

76

CONTINUED LEARNING AND UP-GRADATION OF SKILLS IS THE KEY TO A SUCCESSFUL LIFE IN A GLOBAL COMPETITIVE WORLD

UNESCO sustainable development goal 4.0 "ensure inclusive and equitable quality education and promote lifelong learning opportunities for all by 2030."

"According to the Peace Research Institute in Oslo, the year 2017 was one of the most violent since the end of the Cold War, prolonging the challenge to achieve global peace. Inequality likewise continues to pose problems. Oxfam has raised the alarm about the unbalanced distribution of wealth with 82 percent of the growth in global wealth in 2017 going to the top 1 percent. Meanwhile, 400 million people in Asia and the Pacific region continue to live under US$1.90 a day, 500 million people are undernourished and 136 million children are out of school. In addition, Asia and the Pacific remain highly disaster-prone with 45 percent of global climate change-related disasters between 2011 and 2015 afflicting the region."

"No person or country can solve these problems alone in a fast-globalizing world. Technological advances have intensified and revealed the interconnections between and among people. Actions undertaken in some parts of the planet can affect the well-being and prosperity of millions in other parts. That is why the pursuit of sustainable peace and development requires solidarity, empathy, tolerance, acceptance and a sense of belonging to common humanity – all of which are core elements of GCED"- UNESCO

Core Conceptual Dimensions of Global Citizenship

Education (UNESCO)

1. *To acquire knowledge, understanding, and critical thinking about global, regional, national, and local issues and the interconnectedness and interdependency of different countries and populations.* **io-emotional:**
2. *To have a sense of belonging to common humanity, sharing values and responsibilities, empathy, solidarity, and respect for differences and diversity.*
3. *To act effectively and responsibly at local, national, and global levels for a more peaceful and sustainable world.*

The question reflects the challenge of promoting simultaneously global solidarity and individual or national competitiveness. Global solidarity highlights what education can contribute to the world, while the other focuses on what education can do for individual learners, as an enabler for the acquisition of "21st-century skills". Tension is resolved when the two end results are seen within a continuum. The starting point can be the learners' own interest for their competitiveness, but then they must be redirected, away from their own and local realities, and guided to see the connection of their realities to those of others. As they recognize the mutual impact of their respective realities, they will eventually be empowered to consider the inevitable necessity of mutual cooperation and solidarity. The tension is eased when the interaction, not the gap between the two interests, is emphasized.

What is Global Education System?

It is an education that promotes the core values of global citizenship, namely non-discrimination, respect for diversity, and solidarity for humanity; therefore, its modes of implementation can vary. It can be delivered as an integral part of existing subjects, as much as it can be delivered independently if such is desired, civics, citizenship education, social studies, peace education, or other similar subject areas addressing human rights, democracy, justice, international understanding, etc. While the modality of delivery may not be a major issue, the core values of global citizenship education must be reflected in education policy and the curriculum in order to deliver global citizenship education effectively.

The core benefits of the Global Education System.

The goal of global citizenship education is to empower learners to engage and assume active roles both locally and globally to face and resolve global challenges and ultimately to become proactive contributors to a more just, peaceful, tolerant, inclusive, secure, and sustainable world. Global citizenship education has three conceptual dimensions. The cognitive dimension concerns the learners' acquisition of knowledge, understanding, and critical thinking. The socio-emotional dimension relates to the learners' sense of belonging to common humanity, sharing values and responsibilities, empathy, solidarity, and respect for differences and diversity. The behavioral dimension expects the learners to act responsibly at local, national, and global levels for a more peaceful and sustainable world.

Is there a globally agreed definition of global citizenship?

Global citizenship can be seen as an ethos or a metaphor rather than a formal membership. Being a framework for collective action, global citizenship can and is expected to, generate actions and engagement among, and for, its members through civic actions to promote a better world and future.

When do we start implementing such a program in schools & colleges?

Considering that global citizenship education concerns global affairs and challenges, people tend to think it is an education mainly for "mature" students in post-primary levels. This is not the case. The most challenging dimension to address among the three dimensions of global citizenship education is the socio-emotional dimension that has to do with the formation of attitudes and values. Information and knowledge can be acquired through classroom learning, but values, belief systems, and attitudes are formed through accumulated experiences and socialization processes. They are acquired through the learners' developmental process rather than the schooling process. As such, early childhood is the best place to start with global citizenship education, where early learners acquire the right mindsets for global citizenship.

The fact that local populations have become more heterogeneous, with an increased need for the learners, as part of their civic education, to learn how to live together with those from different cultural and ethnic backgrounds. This is a valid approach and there is no need for a debate on whether this should be called civic education or global citizenship education. Civic education is the most common landing ground of global citizenship education. The same logic should apply to peace education, education for sustainable development or education for international understanding as they advocate for the spirit of global citizenship education. The focus should not be on the naming issue, but on the spirit and core values to be promoted, for which delivery modes, structures as well as labels can vary.

Can we assess to see the impact of GCE and is it only for the Children?

The GCE is relevant to both the students in schools and the elderly y learners in continuous education in the different forms of learning. The cognitive impact will be relatively easy to assess through tests on the students' acquisition of certain sets of information and knowledge. The assessment of the acquisition of socio-emotional and behavioral skills and competencies may require different methods that allow us to measure the development and formation of certain attitudes in students, as well as mindsets and behavioral patterns as part of their development as individuals. To achieve this, participatory assessments will prove useful, such as assignments, demonstrations, observations, projects, and other performance tasks. Notably, the focus of assessment on the impact of global citizenship education should not be on the outcomes, but on the process of learning. In this regard, formative assessments are encouraged over summative assessments.

Global citizenship education is an education that promotes such values as non-discrimination, respect for diversity, and solidarity for humanity. It is not conceptually different from peace education or education for international understanding. Both global citizenship education and education for sustainable development advocate a transformative and holistic pedagogy. Both are concerned with global challenges and actions that are needed to tackle them, while the thematic topics associated with them tend to be specific.

Global citizenship education is more associated with global challenges related to peace and conflict, and education for sustainable development with global challenges related to environmental warnings and natural resources. It is neither constructive nor useful to set global citizenship education and other educational approaches against each other when they are differently labeled efforts targeting related goals and objectives.

What can be taught to be a prominent Global Citizen?

The cognitive dimension of global citizenship education can be addressed through conventional learning combined with learners' accessing and analyzing other sources of information. To address the socio-emotional and behavioral dimensions, however, the pedagogy has to be holistic. Information and knowledge have to be combined with practice. Learners should be provided with actual experiences and opportunities to develop, test, and build their own views, values, and attitudes and to learn how to take actions responsibly. Participation in community activities and opportunities to interact with populations of different backgrounds or of different views are necessary. The core values have to be reflected and practiced in the learners' daily lives in and around the school environment.

Do we need a curriculum for global citizenship education?

Global citizenship education can be delivered by integrating its principles into existing subjects in education. It does not require a new, separate curriculum framework. Curriculum development is also a matter for the national mandate, not one to be framed by an external influence. Considering the varying understandings of the global citizenship concept itself, it is doubtful there can be a globally agreed curriculum framework for global citizenship education. However, global citizenship education is a relatively new term to many experts in curriculum development, practitioners and education managers and there is a need to provide them with some pedagogical guidance. To that effect, UNESCO developed a global guidance document on the overall teaching and learning objectives of global citizenship education4, while leaving the specific ways of achieving those objectives to the discretion of the individual member states. Opportunities for countries to learn about the good practices of other countries are also useful.

The fundamental spirit of global citizenship education should address.

Learning to live together, promotes respect of diversity and solidarity for humanity. This ethos can be practiced globally, but also locally. Teaching students to treat immigrant/migrant children present in the local community with respect and dignity is a valid action for global citizenship education as much as teaching them to learn about cultures outside their national borders. Providing students with opportunities to learn about such fundamental values as non-discrimination and non-violence is a good starting point for global citizenship education. The care for and solidarity with the whole of humanity, those people that one does not know, start with the care for and solidarity with the people one knows. Local challenges and actions constitute valid issues to be addressed by global citizenship education.

UNESCO initiatives on the Global Citizenship Education in the Sustainable Development Goal 4.7

The Global Education First Initiative (GEFI), launched in 2012 by the UN Secretary-General, includes global citizenship education as one of its three priorities, along with access and quality of education. 1 With GEFI, the world education community entered a new era in which education is expected to contribute not only to the fulfilling of individual and national aspirations but also to ensuring the wellbeing of all humanity and the global community. In 2015, global citizenship education was included as one of the topic areas of Target 4.7 of the Sustainable Development Goal on Education that countries must promote and address. These two developments provided the impetus for the world community to pay attention to this particular topic area and emphasize at the policy level for the development of the Nations and its citizens at large.

CHAPTER IX

EQUIPPING THE STUDENTS FOR THE MODERN SCHOOLING SYSTEMS (INFRASTRUCTURE & PERSONAL LEARNING GADGETS)

Information and Communication Technology

Information and Communication Technology is defined as the technologies that enable information access through telecommunication tools such as the internet, mobile phones, television, computer networks, and so on. ICT is not a pedagogy in itself; it is a tool for 21st-century teaching and learning. In our highly connected and rapidly changing world, there is no doubt that the use of ICT is a key aspect of transformative education. At the same time, the proliferation of ICT in every aspect of our lives poses a multitude of social and ethical concerns and issues such as online safety and security (identity theft, scams, hacking, cyberbullying), misuse of information (plagiarism, access to inappropriate contents) and health hazard (game/internet addiction).

Young digital citizens need to equip themselves with the knowledge, skills, and attitudes necessary to take full advantage of the opportunities and be resilient in the face of risks.

Teachers need to know how to use ICT tools appropriately for the content and for safety and security issues.

Benefits of video recordings of all teachings:

The video platform allowed professors to host live classes virtually, complete with real-time speech-to-text transcriptions. It also enabled them to record lectures or class discussions for students to watch and re-watch anytime. That option proved useful for students with unreliable internet access at home, those living in far-away time zones, and those who had trouble following along with professors who were teaching while wearing masks.

For all those reasons, recording those lectures and making them available was the right thing to do, and a significant number of faculty colleagues decided to do that,

Whether their courses have been hybrid, HyFlex (taught in a way that lets each student pick between in-person or online), fully online, or (theoretically) fully in person, many professors have found themselves recording their lectures over the last two years. And even though by now many institutions have moved beyond their early improvised solutions to pandemic challenges, taping lectures has stuck around.

It's a chance that some students like. But some instructors aren't so sure about it—and what it might mean for their teaching strategies, for their privacy or that of their students, or for their intellectual property.

The practice has precedent among proponents of flipped learning, a model that assigns students to watch lectures as homework and reserves class time for interactive activities, sometimes taught that way before the pandemic, when felt it made the most sense for a particular course. It also has supporters among advocates for students with disabilities, who say recorded lectures enable people who have hearing loss, processing difficulties, or other challenges to pause and replay material, or read transcripts, to better understand it and take notes.

Lectures that are recorded can benefit all students. It makes a course inclusive, supportive, and accessible. It brings equity to the course. Everyone is on the same playing field.

Recorded lectures can also help students who miss class because of work or caregiving responsibilities, commuting trouble, or, these days, quarantine requirements due to exposure to COVID-19.

There is a number of reasons a student would have to miss class, yet some professors are worried about what recording their lectures might mean for their teaching practices and course expectations. One fear is that it could make it too tempting for students to skip class for less-pressing reasons. That's a phenomenon that predates the pandemic at medical schools, where many students routinely stay home and watch recordings—sometimes at double the normal speed. Studies about the effects of recorded lectures on student attendance have yielded mixed results.

Also, teaching to a camera instead of a room full of students does not feel the same to many instructors. I do miss those physical, verbal cues that you get when you're in person in a room with people, It's really, really hard to catch that in a Zoom environment, and the video fatigue people go through.

Another point of contention: In an era of heightened tension about academic freedom and "controversial" courses, some instructors are loath to make it easier for their material to escape the classroom and possibly be used against them. Students ripping the videos down and putting them out of context on social media is always a concern.

Privacy for students is another worry. If a classroom is being recorded, students need to know, guidance about getting student consent for recordings and related best practices, which other institutions have requested to use for their own campuses.

And it's not always clear who owns and controls recorded lectures that are hosted and shared through university or third-party ed-tech systems. Colleges can create policies that give them copyright over material that professors record, which has prompted some professors to conceive of scenarios in which they lose their jobs but institutions keep using their recordings.

The University of Michigan has experience navigating intellectual property rights questions thanks in part to its prolific partnership with open-course provider Coursera, It explains that, in general, professors at the university retain ownership of their content and can take it with them if they leave, unless they were specifically hired to produce material exclusive to the institution.

Despite the possible drawbacks, recordings becoming more common, although not required, among professors, students have even come to expect it. The world is moving more and more toward blended learning. The recording of lectures and uploading of lectures is here to stay.

Governments Schools and Colleges must Providing Tech to Students to Shrink the Digital Divide:

When schools and colleges sent students home from campus in the year 2020 due to lockdown on account of the Covid – 19 pandemic, it quickly became clear that some students lacked reliable access to the internet or computers through which to participate in their pandemic-era emergency remote learning.

Institutions did what they could to help at the moment, trying "band-aid remedies" such as loaning out laptops or expanding Wi-Fi service into parking lots, Public gardens, Parks, Railway stations, and many public places.

But administrators realized that the problem they were trying to treat—the digital divide—was less like a mild cut and more like a deep wound. And patching the gash between the technology haves and have-nots might require a more substantial remedy than a band-aid. This was especially evident in many parts of the remote villages in India; with children having no access to the technology, and the so-called Online learning was catering to a mere fraction of the students studying in big cities in private schools and colleges. As per estimates, there are only 17% of Private schools in India in cities and big towns and the rest of the 83% of schools and colleges are in the rural areas run by the state governments, local municipal corporations & villages panchayats.

So this fall, few institutions in many privately deemed Universities are lending iPads and tech accessories including a stylus and smart keyboard to all new freshmen and transfer students who want them, regardless of financial need. The tablets are theirs to hold onto for their entire undergraduate careers.

The Governments must implement 5G connectivity with fiber optic cables across the country, which is fast and reliable, to access especially in remote locations and far-flung hilly areas for the student's learning. The government must also implement schemes for loaning the occasional laptop which is not a new practice in higher education, but providing them en masse may be in state-run schools.

The new efforts are signs that the pandemic's illumination of the digital divide may shift higher education's technology policies away from BYOD—bring your own device—and toward providing tech tools to students, to make sure none is left behind due to having no or even a slow computer or cell phone. Partnerships with some institutions have also been prompted by tech companies looking to better support minority students.

Spotty internet service makes remote learning hard for many college students. So does lacking reliable access to a computer. But even students who do have Wi-Fi and digital devices for schoolwork may not be able to fully participate in their courses if the technology they have is old, outdated, or not powerful enough to handle the demands of today's higher ed software and streaming services.

And that's not only a problem for students trying to do research using, say, advanced statistical packages that take up a lot of computer space. To be able to get a smooth picture and the ability to interact via any of the more common software—Blackboard, Zoom, Teams—you need to have a device that is able to lift and deliver those experiences.

To enjoy full access to digital textbooks, video software, and other online learning systems, college students ideally would have their own, modern computers; you do need a device that is fairly new—not more than five years old. The more mobile the better, so you can take it where you need it and it can connect to Wi-Fi with a modern browser

IT departments have an important role to play in making sure students can fully engage in higher education no matter what devices they have to work with, experts say. Some recommend that departments set and communicate clear standards for technology tools, then establish practices and support systems that bring those standards within reach for every student. For example, instead of asking students to download software that can take up a lot of space on their personal devices, institutions can host those programs on college servers, then allow students to access them remotely via web browsers.

Many universities across the globe are implementing new schemes to further students learning. For example, the California program—officially known as California State University Connectivity Contributing to Equity and Student Success—(CSUCCESS) has several goals, Uhlenkamp says. One is to prepare students for the additional online courses the system is looking to offer even after the pandemic, to meet student demand for remote options. Another is to try to improve graduation rates among low-income students; nearly half of all of the system's undergraduates receive grants.

"We are looking under every rock, examining every process, to help," Uhlenkamp says. "Providing tools to students at the beginning of their career is integral to achieving those goals. It is ensuring all students have an opportunity to graduate."

The program is free for students but costs institutional dollars; California State purchased the iPads, albeit at a discount. If it proves successful, the system hopes to expand it, either with public or private support.

Educators Reflect on a Tough 2021 and Brace for the Future

For many of us, glancing at our social media feeds this year was a rather dispiriting exercise. Learning gaps deepened the pandemic frustrated schools' return to normal and teachers talked openly of burnout and exhaustion when they weren't announcing sudden retirement. It can seem as if the entire system of education is unraveling right when we need it most.

That's not true, of course. Millions of students are still in school, learning as best they can from educators giving everything they've got. As the pandemic's long shadow stretches across a third school year and beyond, schools have—quite literally—entered survival mode

Once again, EdSurge asked educators and leaders from pre-K to higher Ed to reflect on the year we're leaving behind and the one about to dawn. And we asked them not to shy away from harsh realities as they consider what they're letting go of, what they're thinking about differently, and how they're approaching the most urgent challenges.

As ever, our educators did not disappoint, creating a complex tapestry threaded with honesty. They write about guilt, gratitude, making space, and dreaming of new possibilities. They dole out remedies for supporting one another and practicing self-care. And they share what they have learned about finding peace amid the chaos.

"The pandemic has allowed me to be still and know that my role is situational at times. Sometimes I am the conductor and the composer. Other times I am just an alto singing in the choir, and I am OK with that," writes Deitra Colquitt, a school principal, and EdSurge fellow, in an essay about harmony. "I no longer attach value to doing or controlling it all. I am learning to embrace my role at the moment and let the sweet melody of peace ring out.

To move forward we Must Support Educators in Three Key Ways.

The lasting impact of the pandemic has become clearer as students and educators returned to the classroom this year. The gap between the "haves" and "have-nots" has become wider and more acute. Teacher shortages and burnout have risen considerably. And educators, already stretched thin, have been challenged to not only meet all students where they are in their learning but also support their emotional needs as they cope during a crisis.

This moment in education is demanding, and it is also historic. Regardless of your connection to the essential work of education, we have the opportunity to support educators on the frontlines by helping them address three major challenges.

1. *Holding learning technologies accountable.*

With increased Government support to fund technologies in the classroom, expand broadband access, and put devices in the hands of more students, education technology continues to play an important role in the lives of educators and students.

While state- and district-level leaders are investing in technology solutions to help their schools recover and meet students where they are, the problem is that not all ed-tech products are created equal. We must invest in teachers by funding technology solutions proven to meet their needs and improve student learning.

Teachers can only do so much with technology solutions that were rushed through development to market and lack the research demonstrating learning growth. Therefore, education leaders must hold technology solutions to the highest standards of efficacy. Teachers and students should not be test subjects for unproven products.

This means, as education technology providers, it is our obligation to put our solutions under the harshest scrutiny and come prepared with third-party evaluation proving our commitment to student learning growth. Now more than ever, we need to equip teachers with the best tools, and only solutions held to rigorous, independent review should earn the right to support educators and their students.

2. Supporting the learning needs of teachers and students today, not just preparing for the assessments of tomorrow.

The most effective learning tools and resources should complement classroom lessons and empower teachers to engage each student with personalized learning experiences. We need to move beyond tools that teach to a test and instead focus on solutions that equip educators with real-time student data and training that enables them to better connect with each of their students right now.

To do this, we need to first ensure classroom technologies do not create more work for teachers. Rather, ed-tech should encourage and challenge each student to deeply learn skills until proficiency by adapting to their individual learning.

While students are learning from mistakes and challenging themselves to develop a curiosity for learning, ed-tech is providing teachers real-time student learning data with actionable recommendations that go beyond test scores. When combined with their own student observations, these recommended next steps and lessons give teachers a more complete view of when and how to differentiate for students.

It's also the responsibility of education technology partners and school districts to provide continuous, job-embedded professional development relevant to teachers' learning needs.

This pandemic has placed immense pressure on teachers to quickly adapt. We must look at teachers as learners themselves to support them today as well as when the pandemic eases and teachers are ushered into a new world with new definitions of schooling, new expectations of learning technologies and new levels of partnership with home-based learning guardians. In partnership, we can ensure teachers are best supported to personalize instruction for individual students and small groups

3. Partnering with schools to adapt to the social and emotional needs of teachers and students.

When discussing the needs of teachers and students, we can't ignore mental health. Teachers are leaving the profession at an alarming rate and are experiencing high levels of job-related stress and depression. Students are also being challenged by these difficult times and coping with increased stress and trauma, requiring more one-on-one attention from their teachers. Educators and their students cannot recover from the pandemic if we don't support their social and emotional learning needs—first.

We have to go beyond acknowledging the crisis exists. Educators should be given strategies to create safe, connected learning environments. School and district leaders should implement professional development and staff retreats that put mental and physical well-being in focus. Additionally, social-emotional learning efforts must recognize the social injustices experienced by people of color in our communities and how the pandemic worsened these already inequitable conditions.

Education technologies and providers also play a role in this essential work. Not only can we build social-emotional learning tools into our services, but we can also understand our partners are prioritizing mental health and well-being.

There are big challenges ahead, but I am optimistic that the future of learning is bright because of the dedication from our educators and students. By continuously listening and adapting to their needs today, together we help tackle these immediate hurdles with solutions that pave a more equitable education path for all students moving forward.

CHAPTER X

MORE EMPHASIS ON GECD FOR A CONDUCIVE & INCLUSIVE SOCIETY IN THE 21ST CENTURY

UNESCO, Global Citizenship Education.

Target 4.7 indicates that by 2030 all learners will "acquire knowledge and skills needed to promote sustainable development, including among others through education for sustainable development and sustainable lifestyles, human rights, gender equality, promotion of a culture of peace and non-violence, global citizenship, and appreciation of cultural diversity and of culture's contribution to sustainable development."

UNESCO, Global Citizenship Education (GCED) is an educational approach that nurtures respect and solidarity in learners in order to build a sense of belonging to common humanity and help them become responsible and active global citizens in building inclusive and peaceful societies. GCED, combined with Education for Sustainable Development (ESD), converges in Target 4.7 of Sustainable Development Goal 4.0 on Education of the 2030 Agenda for Sustainable Development.

Since its emergence in the global discourse on education (2012), GCED has been a contested concept. For some, it is perceived as dissociated from local needs and realities, while for others it is a timely approach that underlines the need to sharpen the relevance of education. Tensions and debates around GCED have been particularly intense in contexts where the words 'global' or 'globalization' are misconstrued as referring to processes that are exogenous to their societies -- for instance, with globalization being equated with "westernization".

All the while, UNESCO has observed that many countries and societies have national/local/traditional concepts that promote ideas that echo those at the core of GCED. These local concepts resonate with the three notions that distinguish GCED from other educational approaches:

- Respect for diversity.
- Solidarity.
- A shared sense of humanity.

These concepts are rooted in local cosmogonies, founding stories, and national histories, and they can often be found in constitutions, national anthems, and government policy documents, as well as in the writings of historical figures ("founding fathers and mothers").

Unfortunately, these concepts are sometimes insufficiently known and celebrated beyond their regions of origin. They are also sometimes insufficiently valued as meaningful starting points to teach and learn about GCED in ways that are locally relevant.

As societies and economies undergo deep transformations and face new challenges, new forms of education are called for to foster the knowledge, skills, and values that learners need to thrive, prosper, and become resilient. Moreover, in today's world, amidst the global health pandemic, the importance of building resilience in the education systems is underscored, as education is recognized to have an increasing role in building peace, sustainable development, greater justice, social equity, and gender equality – in short about learning to live together on a planet under pressure.

With the growing attention and efforts to promote GCED policy and practice in the Asia-Pacific region, and to synergies the diverse regional efforts from partners who have been active in implementing GCED and GCED related programs and activities, the Asia-Pacific Regional GCED Network was launched in May 2018 Jakarta, Indonesia. Hereinafter referred to as the Network. The Network brings various organizations committed to the realization of GCED towards Education 2030. It creates opportunities for GCED stakeholders (i.e. policymakers, researchers, educators) to gather and exchange information and research, share good practices, discuss challenges and identify gaps of GCED, suggest possible solutions, and provide expertise.

Since 2018, The Network has been actively supporting the regional efforts in GCED promotion and implementation. Each year, various activities are designed and carried out by the collective efforts within the Network and in collaboration with other partners. In 2021, UNESCO Bangkok and the Asia-Pacific Centre of Education for International Understanding (APCEIU) the co-chairs of the Network invited two Network core working group members, the Korean Society of Education for International Understanding (KOSEIU) and the Japan Association for International Education (JAIE) to host the first online forum for the Network, as a launch of the "member-hosted online forum" to further synergize the Network and its members.

The COVID-19 global pandemic continues to remind us that we, as common humanity, are strongly interconnected and yet vulnerable. Learning remains interrupted in many countries in the region. Many children and youth, who are at the heart of GCED, have been cut off from learning as well as the supportive and safe school environment. They may also have been exposed to misinformation, hate speech, violence, etc. Therefore, more resilience shall be built in the minds of students, parents, educators, and so on.

Objectives

The online forum aspires to share good practices of curriculum and pedagogy, stimulate dialogue on how teaching and learning need to be reviewed and adapted in facing the challenges brought by the COVID-19 global pandemic. To contribute towards building resilient education systems, the ultimate objective is to inspire and empower teachers/educators in teaching and learning in response to emerging challenges.

The outcome of this exercise should result in benefits to all.

- Enable knowledge exchange and dissemination of good practices to enhance the quality of Education in Asia and the Pacific;
- Encourage teachers and education experts to engage in dialogue to promote and utilize evidence to inform policy and practices;
- Improve curriculum and teacher training to contribute towards building the resilience of education systems in the aftermath of the pandemic;
- Establish a community of practice and collaboration among countries.

Beneficiaries/Participants

The direct beneficiaries will be network members, including officials from states (i.e., Ministry of Education) teaching professionals, and research institutions. Other beneficiaries will be stakeholders, learners, teachers, school leaders, and their families.

The goal of curriculum development is to foster global citizenship. Therefore, we have to create a curriculum centered on learning-based the national curriculum, we have to engage in learning activities systematically and continuously that foster global citizenship.

In international understanding learning, by knowing cultures of each other's countries, students fostered a tolerant attitude to each other's differences, and by knowing what's happening in the world, they fostered developing a sense of commitment to global issues and multifaceted perspective.

In community understanding learning, by knowing about the town where they live, students rediscovered their town and fostered attachment to the town where they live. Furthermore, by knowing that the town is supported by various people, students will be aware that they will support the town in the future.

Through this curriculum development, the students find four perspectives to foster global citizenship. "Respect themselves and their friend" "Know about their community" "Know the diversity of the world" "Notice that the world is connected" Learning activities that are conscious of these four perspectives will be important points in creating a curriculum that fosters global citizenship systematically and continuously.

As a way to seek a new role and presence of GCED under the Covid-19 pandemic situation, the presentation should focus on how GCED can help with subjects to develop relevance in today's world. More specifically, the presentation shall showcase how project-based learning in schools. English class has dealt with such issues as overcoming hatred around the world, discerning facts from fake news through media literacy, developing appropriate technologies for the developing countries without proper online platforms, etc. In case of blended learning, which stands for utilizing both online learning and offline classes concurrently, has been widespread under the pandemic situation. The presentation will provide examples of how blended learning methods can effectively be utilized in order to develop classroom modules on GECD.

UNESCO initiatives through the Indian Government:

In India, a category One Research Institute of UNESCO has already created a Global Citizenship Curriculum which can transform the way we teach (MGIEP) Mahatma Gandhi Institute of Education for Peace and Sustainable Development a government research institute in India has initiated the curriculum to incorporate in the learning framework titled EMCC of EMC2 aimed to build empathy, mindfulness, compassion and critical inquiry in students.

Social and Emotional Learning (SEL)- can be broadly defined as the process of acquiring the competencies, skills, and/or attitudes to recognize and manage emotions, develop caring and concern for others, establish positive relationships, make responsible decisions, and handle challenging situations

Research from the neurosciences has also shown that these biological roots of rage and aggression can be trained using behavioral tools of SEL and redirected towards peaceful and constructive action. This retraining of brain circuits happens because of a remarkable process called neuroplasticity, which is the ability of the brain to rewire itself by repeated training and practice. Specifically, building competencies of attention regulation through programs on mindfulness (Davidson et al., 2003) and emotional regulation – which build positive peer relationships (Obsuth et al., 2015), and compassion – has been shown to regulate and reduce aggression and violence, and promote peaceful and pro-social behavior.

For instance, in India alone, about 25% of children between the ages of 13 and 15 suffer from some form of depression or anxiety. The highly competitive nature of the present education system, the growing uncertainty of the employment market, and the types of jobs that will be in demand in the future have been mentioned as some of the major causes for the growing levels of stress and anxiety, at the same time, research from the learning sciences tells us that the same knowledge and behaviors that contribute towards reduced aggression, violence, anxiety, fear and anger also contribute towards improved academic success. The competencies of attention regulation and emotional regulation improve with such knowledge, leading to improvement in learning. the key findings summarized above indicate that the introduction of SEL can in fact provide a double dividend to learners and the society in the form of improving academic achievements and also nurturing empathic and compassionate individuals dedicated to building peaceful and sustainable societies across the world.

Conclusion:

It is thus urgent and necessary that this new knowledge and understanding be mainstreamed into education systems to transform the systems with the purpose of shaping a future that embraces and facilitates improved academic success as well as peace and human flourishing.

MGIEP's important initiatives in Social and Emotional Learning

The key components of an (SEL) –Social and Emotional Learning framework should include critical inquiry, focus attention, regulate emotion and cultivate compassionate action to produce a balance of intrapersonal, interpersonal, and cognitive competencies while always ensuring that these frameworks are grounded in empirical evidence.

Humans are born with an innate capacity for forming social connections. Humans need social and emotional connections for learning and higher-order cognition. Learning is facilitated or hindered by the social and emotional experiences of the learner. Therefore, an individual's emotional and social development is as important as the individual's cognitive and biological development. Education systems must be able to address and contribute to this aspect of the human experience.

A growing body of scientific research indicates that students' social and emotional competence not only predicts their school success, but also predicts a range of important outcomes in late adolescence and adulthood, including high school graduation, postsecondary completion, employment, financial stability, physical health, and overall mental health and well-being.

There is a confluence of research from multiple studies showing that students who participate in SEL programs, relative to students who do not, demonstrate significantly improved social and emotional competencies, attitudes, and behavioral adjustment. In addition, they also outperformed those students who did not participate in SEL programs, on indices of academic achievement by 11-percentile points. Using extrapolative methods, preliminary results using data from over 60 countries suggest that the productivity lost for not spending on SEL interventions is about 29% of the Gross National Income.

Early childhood and adolescence constitute periods of maximal sensitivity of the brain to experience and to the environment.

However, brain development, cognitive social, and emotional developments are dynamic and non-linear. Therefore, enriched social environments and social interactions have a positive effect on brain maturation as well as on cognitive social, and emotional development at all ages.

Digital Technology in Social and Emotional Learning (SEL)

The digital innovation in the field of education during the past 20 years offers the option of scaling up SEL to reach the millions of learners within and beyond classrooms. Digital games, if designed with research-based pedagogical properties, can plant the seeds that can transform attitudes, knowledge, and skills in a socially and politically complex time. Indeed, games can propel social and emotional learning by offering deep, experiential learning opportunities that draw on students' active and creative engagement. However, the potential depends upon the design of the environments wherein those digital tools that are deployed provide a ripe opportunity for social and emotional skill development. They provide a safe space to express ideas, experiment with solutions, and obtain feedback on sensitive issues.

In addition to digital tools, educators need to incorporate activities for student reflection, classroom discussions, and other projects to deepen learning. Students should move between the digital tool and face-to-face interaction with peers and adults and individual work (self-reflecting, writing, and creating) across the unit.

Who Can Best Implement SEL?

Teachers are primary exemplars for social and emotional learning as they are central figures in the socialization of children and serve as important role models for their students. To promote learning, teachers must find ways to meet the immediate social and learning needs of individual students in complex, frequently under-resourced educational environments.

Teachers must recognize how their own behavior models SEL concepts and competencies through their students' behavioral observational learning, which may be more powerful than the curriculum. In addition, teachers must have a good understanding of their students in order to deliver SEL programs effectively and to apply the content knowledge to classroom interactions and events as they naturally occur in the classroom. Teachers must also model appropriate social behavior and impact classroom dynamics directly and indirectly by taking actions to manage or modify the social networks emerging in their classroom. These include peer norms, status hierarchies, and social affiliation patterns that can have a powerful effect on classroom environments.

CHAPTER XI

HOW SHOULD THE ELDERLY & THE DISADVANTAGED COPE UP WITH THE CHANGING TECHNOLOGICAL DEVELOPMENTS?

The impact of changing technology on the elderly.

The elderly will be a square peg in a round hole in this changing technological world, access to the new gadgets and knowledge of the advancing AI functionalities will be a big handicap due to lack of knowledge and skills, the driving AI functionalities will be performing a greater number of tasks, and multiple complex situations, performing tasks at a faster pace, of the preferences and choices we make in everyday life. The expected population in any country with the life expectancy reaching higher age limits, the disadvantaged will be in the ratio of 25% to 30% of the population of the country, especially in the developed and developing countries, putting a burden on the economy of the countries. The divide in the poor countries will almost be in the same ratio though the life expectancy is less, the school dropouts will continue to be higher, who will not be technologically in sync with the current environment.

UNESCO Recommendations on Adult Learning and Education (RALE)

Adult Education by 2030 Framework for Action, defines adult learning and education as a *'core component of lifelong learning, and highlights 'learning for active citizenship' as one of the three key domains of adult learning and education. Such learning is achieved through 'what is variously known as community, popular or liberal education. Learning opportunities for active citizenship are expected to empower adult learners 'to actively engage with social issues such as poverty, gender, intergenerational solidarity, social mobility, justice, equity, exclusion, violence, unemployment, environmental protection, and climate change'* (UNESCO and UIL, 2016, p. 7).

ALE and GCED, when interpreted in a specific, non-neutral way (i.e. to address social transformation, equity, and social justice from a non-Western viewpoint), share a number of structural and central elements.

First, global citizenship responsibilities apply to everyone, of all ages, genders, and backgrounds. However, youth and adults have an advantage over other age groups with regard to actively engaging locally in their immediate communities and globally because they occupy multiple roles (e.g. as voters, consumers, waste producers, volunteers, spouses, parents, careers, workers, employers) that involve some kind of cultural, social and political representation. Second, people learn throughout their lives and in multiple environments that support new learning (i.e. the acquisition of knowledge, skills, and capacities for sense-making, forming judgments, and making informed decisions).

However, learning does not happen in a social vacuum and is never free or disconnected from people's commitments and values, a key component of adult learning and education. It involves a continuum of learning and proficiency levels which allows citizens to engage in lifelong learning and participate fully in the community, workplace, and wider society. It includes the ability to read and write, to identify, understand, interpret, create, communicate and compute, using printed and written materials, as well as the ability to solve problems in an increasingly technological and information-rich environment.

Literacy is an essential means of building people's knowledge, skills, and competencies to cope with the evolving challenges and complexities of life, culture, economy, and society. When unpacking this definition, the following key features can be identified: literacy is related to the written language; it is a means of communication and of participation in society; it includes problem-solving in environments that are increasingly shaped by ICTs, and it involves a learning continuum comprising different proficiency levels. The acquisition of literacy does not only involve knowledge (e.g. of the alphabet, script, and language) and skills (e.g. reading fluency and comprehension), but touches also on attitudes, dispositions, and motivation (e.g. confident and self-sufficient learners are more likely to use their literacy skills broadly), as well as on values (e.g. to critically assess the purpose of a message, or to use social media responsibly in order to interact with different audiences.

Literacy acquisition involves learning the 'code' (the alphabet), making meaning, and thinking critically. It is about linking spoken language with written language (text), decoding and encoding written forms of language, developing (phonological) awareness of sounds and words, and learning about and applying conventions of written language. Meaning-making is only possible if this applies beyond the literal level by analyzing meanings, responding to (different types of) texts critically, and reasonably. This in turn requires both the continuous development of higher levels of literacy proficiency and advanced language proficiency. Understanding the complex interrelationships between literacy, language, and learning is a prerequisite for designing and implementing meaningful learning activities that are focused on global citizenship topics. Nowadays, information is often accessed, analyzed, and communicated via the Internet using digital devices and applications, such as personal computers, tablets, and smartphones. The increasing importance of digital competencies (i.e. problem-solving in technology-rich environments) has added to the complexity of literacy.

This issue must be addressed within the dynamics of the multifaceted interrelationship of what the Organization for Economic Co-operation and Development (OECD) refers to as the 'key information-processing competencies (i.e. literacy, numeracy, language and problem-solving in technology-rich environments) that are relevant to adults in many 21st Century contexts, and which are needed in order for them to fully participate in social-economic, cultural and civic life.

The overall goal of the SDGs, 'to transform our world', also applies to the field of adult literacy. Literacy should be seen as a social practice with transformative potential. This potential, however, can only be realized if we embrace lifelong learning.

This involves:

1. Understanding literacy is a continuous learning process that takes place across all ages and generations.
2. Embedding literacy (and numeracy) in or combining it with the development of other skills and integrating it into other development activities.
3. Ensuring that learning always centers on content, which ranges from working with words that generate reflection and discussions, to reading complex texts about themes that are relevant to learners.

Hence, the integration of content or a 'subject matter' – such as global citizenship topics – into literacy provision reflects the fundamental principles of any literacy teaching and learning approach. Adult literacy programs from around the world typically pursue a multiplicity of objectives and address a broad range of learning content.

Moreover, in a number of cases, literacy development is not flagged as the key purpose of a program, but is rather 'embedded' in one or more of its main goals (e.g. to culturally and linguistically empower an ethnic minority; or to equip people to cope with natural disasters). It is thus important to take note of the huge diversity of adult education programs involving literacy and numeracy components: these can be formal (i.e. equivalency programs leading to recognized primary and secondary school certificates) or non-formal; of shorter or longer duration; focus on the development of basic or advanced proficiency levels; and be oriented towards general, vocational and/or 'life skills' themes All of these programs are, in principle, able to address global citizenship issues and SDG 4.7 themes effectively.

Advantages of having literate elders:

While an approach that views literacy as a social practice defines reading and writing as skills that are re harnessed in order to connect people in local contexts with the wider world. In other words, as people become more literate, they become able to engage in different ways with the world beyond their own villages and communities. Such a process reflects the goal of GCED, namely to empower learners to engage and assume active roles both locally and globally to face and resolve global challenges' Furthermore, improving male literacy also has a positive impact on women's political participation. It is believed that this will attribute to the fact that literate men are more likely to vote for women candidates and, as party leaders, to field women candidates.

A recent study on two major adult literacy campaigns implemented in South Africa –illustrates the way in which literacy interventions can help to enhance the quality of life of vulnerable communities. The social assets and connections emerging from both campaigns show a network of agency and resilience in some of the country's poor, rural communities.

Evidence-based learners' feedback reflecting on the outcomes of their participation in the campaign shows the critical role that literacy interventions played in fostering community cohesion and peaceful co-existence. Bringing together people with common problems in literacy learning groups enabled them to collectively develop strategies to address the challenges they faced. The process of becoming literate enhanced learners' confidence and, by extension, their social and political participation

Adult educators need to be able to use a variety of information sources, as they may interface with learners in person or via digital and mediated spaces created by information and communication technologies (ICTs). Hence, the systematic use of ICTs is an important way of extending the coverage of ALE programs by providing learners and educators alike with relevant training opportunities. 'Digital citizenship' should thus be focused on and the importance of media and information competence cannot be overemphasized at a time when a worldwide rise in 'nationalist perspectives' has been observed Like everyone else, adult educators may have gained skills through formal, non-formal, and/or informal learning in a wide range of settings. The quality of ALE courses automatically improves when adult educators are required to hold a prior qualification and are provided with high-quality training in the form of pre-service, in-service, and ongoing training programs.

Moreover, RALE calls for flexible and seamless learning pathways between formal and non-formal education and training; and the provision of learning environments conducive to quality adult learning and education, validation, and accreditation of all forms of learning outcomes is a practice that makes visible and values the full range of competencies (knowledge, skills, and attitudes) that individuals have obtained through various means in different phases and contexts of their lives.

Requirements at the national level:

• GCED, like all issues that the 2030 Agenda seeks to tackle, is cross-sectoral in nature, particularly when the diverse settings and multiple actors involved in ALE are taken into account. Consequently, there is a need for reflection and interventions to determine.

(i) how providers other than national ministries of education (i.e. groups and bodies specializing in youth, women's affairs, social affairs, labor, and employment, etc.) can be sensitized to GCED,

(ii) how GCED can be made relevant to these sources of ALE.

• There should be a guiding framework to define GCED, describe GCED-related competencies, and broadly outline how GCED could permeate ALE programs. This framework could, for example, be established in the context of a forum in which education actors, practitioners, and stakeholders agree on a meaningful definition of GCED dependent on the national context, and identify ways of strengthening

GCED in ALE programs. Whatever form this process takes, there should be a broad consensus as to the desirability of GCED, how it should be conveyed, and how real-life opportunities can be created to put GCED into practice. This consensus should in turn lead to the development of a context-sensitive to mainstream GCED in ALE.

• National authorities should promote minimum qualifications and training for ALE educators, and that training should equip educators with the fundamentals of how to convey GCED-related content in their lessons.

• Educators should be able to access a national database of GCED-related materials and resources. Bearing in mind that providers' coverage is fragmented, and the fact that these providers are likely to take on a project-based approach to GCED, a database of documents would expand the life cycle of materials Produced beyond the initial project for which they were developed.

• Bearing in mind that ALE relies largely on the initiative of CSOs and communities, it seems essential to cultivate a positive attitude towards CSOs. In addition, incentives should be developed to encourage CSOs to integrate GCED into the ALE programs they implement.

• Data is an important component of policy-related decision-making and accountability. The SDG monitoring framework foresees both a global indicator and thematic indicators to measure progress towards the mainstreaming of GCED and education for sustainable development. However, aside from not having a global remit, not all current monitoring tools take the diversity of ALE into account. Countries are thus obliged to develop/enrich their own statistics where ALE is concerned if they wish to measure both the provision of GCED-related content and the GCED-related knowledge learner's gain. Defining relevant measurement tools will entail defining context-relevant concepts and outcomes related to GCED in ALE.

INSTRUCTORS:

The (basic and advanced) training that course instructors receive is fundamental to the course's success. A master's degree or partial qualification in ALE, as well as proven qualifications and experience in the fields of literacy and basic education, are a prerequisite. GCED may not be central to these qualifications but is nonetheless covered by several of their constituent components. Instructors must be willing to participate in further education and training as part of the project. Course leaders undergo further compulsory training on democracy-building, internal differentiation,9 dealing with traumatized refugees, and intercultural competencies.

(a) Cognitive domain: Cognitive learning goals, especially those related to communication, is pursued primarily through language promotion. Course participants come from a variety of backgrounds; courses should therefore be designed flexibly so they can be adapted to different learning needs. Respect for diversity and heterogeneity is promoted, as is intercultural understanding. In addition, further subject-related content is acquired through internships. Democratic values and knowledge about living (together) in Germany are integral to providing participants with basic political education.

(b) Socio-emotional domain: This domain focuses particularly on fostering empathy, respect, and solidarity. BEF Alpha promotes these skills through its courses and internships. Course participants learn to react to cultural differences with respect and empathy. References to childcare have proven valuable in drawing attention to course content on health, nutrition, hygiene, and sex education.

(c) Behavioural domain: During the courses and internships, participants should learn to establish and adhere to community rules so that they can take on responsibilities for that community and guarantee good learning outcomes. By learning about basic rights, the social system, and other support services, participants should become familiar with and know how to make use of the possibilities available to them.

BEF Alpha furthermore attaches great importance to the promotion of equal rights in line with UNESCO's overarching priorities in particular the rights of women who are at a severe disadvantage as regards education and decision-making in the family. BEF Alpha makes a significant contribution to gender equality by providing basic political education while pursuing the goals of GCED.

List Of Acronyms:

APCEIU Asia-Pacific Centre of Education for International Understanding

ASPnet Associated Schools Project Network (UNESCO)

EAG Experts Advisory Group

ECOWAS Economic Community of West African States

ESC Education for Social Cohesion

ESD Education for Sustainable Development

GCED Global Citizenship Education

GEFI Global Education First Initiative (of the UN Secretary-General)

GIZ Deutsche Gesellschaft für Internationale Zusammenarbeit GmbH

HIV/AIDS Human Immunodeficiency Virus/ Acquired Immune Deficiency Syndrome

HQ Headquarters

IBE International Bureau of Education (UNESCO)

ICT Information and Communication Technology

IEA International Association for the Evaluation of Educational Achievement

KEDI Korean Educational Development Institute

KICE Korea Institute for Curriculum and Evaluation

LMTF Learning Metrics Task Force

LTLT Learning to Live Together

MGIEP Mahatma Gandhi Institute of Education for Peace and Sustainable Development

NGO Non-Governmental Organization

OHCHR Office of the United Nations High Commissioner for Human Rights

OSCE/ODIHR Organization for Security and Co-operation in Europe/Office for Democratic Institutions and Human Rights

PEIC Protect Education in Insecurity and Conflict

SDGs Sustainable Development Goals

UIS UNESCO Institute for Statistics

UN United Nations

UK United Kingdom

UNEP United Nations Environment Programme

UNESCO United Nations Educational, Scientific and Cultural Organization

UNICEF United Nations Children's Fund

<u>ACRONYMS USED IN THE INDIAN CONTEXT:</u>

AAR Age-Specific Attendance Rate

ABL Activity Based Learning

AIE Alternative and Innovative Education

AIES All India Education Survey

AIMMP Area Intensive and Madrasa Modernisation Programme

AIPEBM Area Intensive Programme for Educationally Backward Minorities

ANAR Adjusted Net Attendance Rate ANER Adjusted Net Enrolment Rate

AP Andhra Pradesh

APL Above Poverty Level

ASER Annual Status of Education Report

ASHA Accredited Social Health Activist

AWC Anganwadi Centre AWPB Annual Work Plan and Budget

AWW Anganwadi Worker BaLA Building as Learning Aid

BEO Block Education Officer

BIMARU Bihar, Madhya Pradesh, Rajasthan, and Uttar Pradesh

BPL Below Poverty Line BRC Block Resource Centre

BRCC Block Resource Centre Coordinator

ABE Central Advisory Board of Education

CAG Comptroller and Auditor General of India CAL Computer Aided Learning

CCE Continuous and Comprehensive Evaluation

CEDAW Committee on the Elimination of Discrimination Against Women

CLIP Children Language Improvement Programme
CMF Conceptual and Methodological Framework
CMR Child Mortality Rate
CORD Collaborative and Research Dissemination
CRC Cluster Resource Centre
CRCC Cluster Resource Centre Coordinator
CRPF Central Reserve Police Force
CSR Corporate Social Responsibility
CSS Centrally Sponsored Scheme
CTS Child Tracking Survey
CWSN Children With Special Needs
DEO District Education Office
DIET District Institute of Education and Training
DISE District Information System for Education xvii
DPC District Project Coordinator
DPEP District Primary Education Programme
EBBs Educationally Backward Blocks
ECCE Early Childhood Care and Education
ECD Early Childhood Development
ECE Early Childhood Education
EDCIL Educational Consultants India Ltd.
EFA Education for All
EGS Education Guarantee Scheme
GDP Gross Domestic Product
GER Gross Enrolment Ratio GoI Government of India
GPI Gender Parity Index
HDI Human Development Index
ICDS Integrated Child Development Services
IDMI Infrastructure Development for Minority Institutions
IHDS India Human Development Survey
IIPS International Institute for Population Sciences
ILO International Labour Organization
IMF-WEO International Monetary Fund-World Economic Outlook
IMR Infant Mortality Rate

IPEC International Programme of Elimination of Child Labour
ISCED International Standard Classification of Education
JRM Joint Review Mission
KGBV Kasturba Gandhi Balika Vidyalaya
LEHAR Learning Enhancement Activities in Rajasthan
LEP Learning Enhancement Programme
CD Municipal Corporation of Delhi
MCS Model Cluster School
MDGs Millennium Development Goals
MDM Mid Day Meal
MEO Mandal Education Officer
MHRD Ministry of Human Resource Development
MLE Multi-Lingual Education
MME Modernisation of Madrasa Education
MMR Maternal Mortality Rate MoI Medium of Instruction
MP Madhya Pradesh
MPCE Monthly Per Capita Expenditure
MS Mahila Samakhya MTA Mother Teacher Associations
MWCD Ministry of Women and Child Development
NCAER National Council of Applied Economic Research
NCDHR National Campaign on Dalit Human Rights xviii
NCERT National Council of Education Research and Training
NCF National Curriculum Framework
NCFTE National Curriculum Framework of Teacher Education
NCLP National Child Labour Project
NCPCR National Commission for Protection of Child Rights
NCTE National Council for Teacher Education
NER Net Enrolment Ratio
NFE Non-formal Education
NFHS National Family Health Survey
NGO Non-Government Organisation
NHE Nutrition and Health Education
NIPCCD National Institute of Public Cooperation and Child Development

NMCME National Monitoring Committee on Minorities Education

NPE National Policy on Education

NPEGEL National Programme for Education of Girls at Elementary Level

NP-NSPE National Programme of Nutrition Support to Primary Education

NRBC Non-Residential Bridge Course

NSSO National Sample Survey Organisation

NUEPA National University of Educational Planning and Administration

OB Operation Blackboard

OOSC Out-of-School children

PAB Project Approval Board

PAISA Planning, Allocation, and Expenditure, Institutions: Studies in Accountability

POA Plan of Action

PP Purchasing Power Parity

PRI Panchayati Raj Institution

PSE Preschool Education

PTA Parent Teacher Association

PTR Pupil-Teacher Ratio

PWD Person With Disabilities

QMT Quality Monitoring Tools

RBC Residential Bridge Course

RTE Right to Education

SAIES Seventh All India Education Survey

SC Scheduled Caste

SCERT State Council of Education Research and Training

SCPCR State Commission for Protection of Child Rights

SCR Student-Classroom Ratio

SDP School Development Plan

SEMIS Secondary Education Management Information System

SES Selected Education Statistics

SIS State Implementation Societies xix

LIST OF ACRONYMS:

SMC School Management Committee
SMDC School Management Development Committee
SNA System of National Accounting
SPQEM Scheme for Providing Quality Education in Madrasas
SRI-IMRB Social and Rural Research Institute – International Marketing Research Bureau SSA Sarva Shiksha Abhiyan
SSE Statistics of School Education
SSHE Sanitation and Hygiene Education Programme
ST Scheduled Tribe
STC Special Training Centres
TET Teacher Eligibility Test
TLM Teaching Learning Material
UDISE Unified District Information System for Education
UEE Universal Elementary Education
UIS UNESCO Institute for Statistics
UNDP United Nations Development Programme
UNESCO United Nations Educational, Scientific and Cultural Organization
UNICEF United Nation's Children Fund
UNPD United Nations Population Division
UP Uttar Pradesh
US United States
UT Union Territory
VEC Village Education Committees
VER Village Education Register
WSDP Whole School Development Plan

www.ingramcontent.com/pod-product-compliance
Lightning Source LLC
Chambersburg PA
CBHW061346160726
47995CB00001B/197